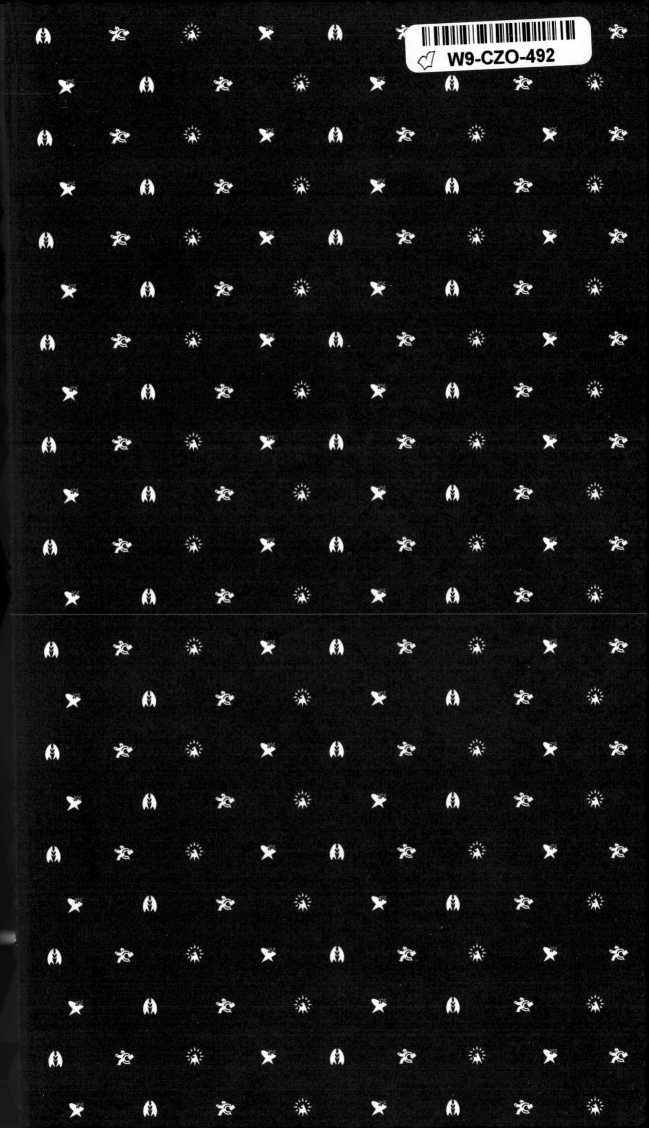

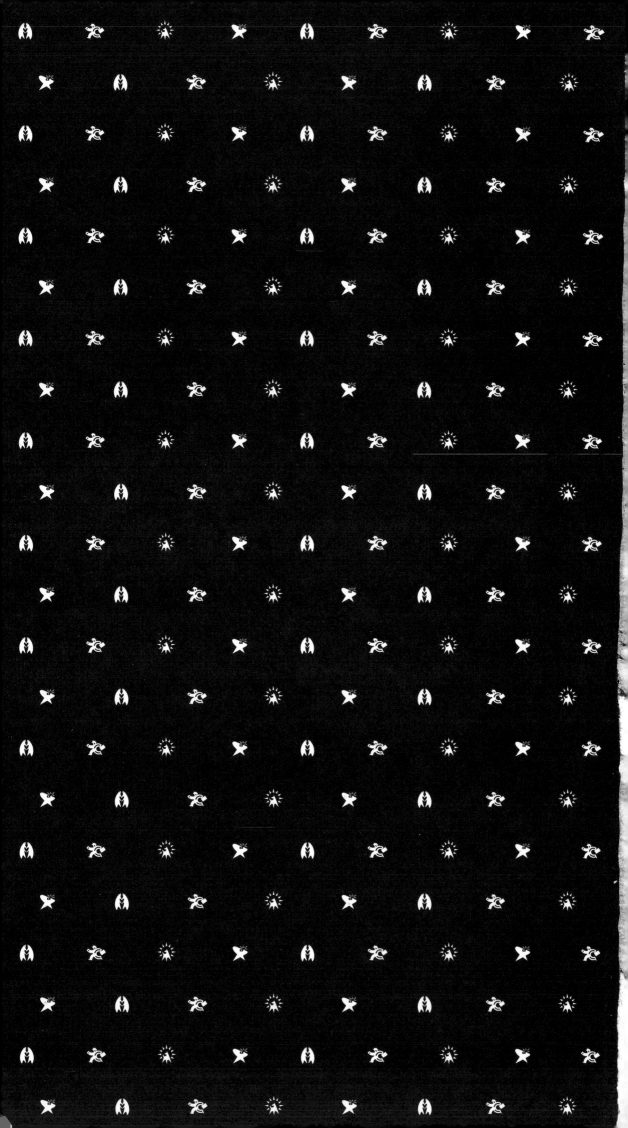

GRAPHIS LOGO 3

GRAPHIS LOGO 3

THE INTERNATIONAL COLLECTION OF LOGO DESIGN

LOGOGESTALTUNG IM INTERNATIONALEN ÜBERBLICK

UNE COMPILATION INTERNATIONALE SUR LE DESIGN DE LOGOS

EDITED BY · HERAUSGEGEBEN VON · EDITÉ PAR:

B. MARTIN PEDERSEN

PUBLISHER AND CREATIVE DIRECTOR: B. MARTIN PEDERSEN

EDITORS: HEINKE JENSSEN, ANNETTE CRANDALL

ASSOCIATE EDITORS: PEGGY CHAPMAN, JÖRG REIMANN

ART DIRECTORS: B. MARTIN PEDERSEN, JENNIFER THORPE

GRAPHIS U.S., INC, NEW YORK.

GRAPHIS PRESS CORP. ZÜRICH (SWITZERLAND)

Contents · Inhalt · Sommaire

REMARKS

WE EXTEND OUR HEARTFELT THANKS TO CONTRIBUTORS THROUGHOUT THE WORLD WHO HAVE MADE
IT POSSIBLE TO PUBLISH A WIDE AND INTERNATIONAL SPECTRUM OF THE BEST WORK IN THIS FIELD.
ENTRY INSTRUCTIONS FOR ALL GRAPHIS BOOKS MAY BE REQUESTED AT:
GRAPHIS PRESS, 141 LEXINGTON AVENUE, NEW YORK, NY 10016-8193

ANMERKUNGEN

UNSER DANK GILT DEN EINSENDERN AUS ALLER WELT, DIE ES UNS ERMÖGLICHT HABEN, EIN BREI-
TES, INTERNATIONALES SPEKTRUM DER BESTEN ARBEITEN ZU VERÖFFENTLICHEN.
TEILNAHMEBEDINGUNGEN FÜR DIE GRAPHIS-BÜCHER SIND ERHÄLTLICH BEIM:
GRAPHIS VERLAG AG, DUFOURSTRASSE 107, 8008 ZÜRICH, SCHWEIZ

REMERCIEMENTS

NOUS REMERCIONS LES PARTICIPANTS DU MONDE ENTIER QUI ONT RENDU POSSIBLE LA PUBLICA-
TION DE CET OUVRAGE OFFRANT UN PANORAMA COMPLET DES MEILLEURS TRAVAUX.
LES MODALITÉS D'INSCRIPTION PEUVENT ÊTRE OBTENUES AUPRÈS DE:
EDITIONS GRAPHIS, DUFOURSTRASSE 107, 8008 ZÜRICH, SUISSE

(PRECEDING SPREAD) ART DIRECTOR: CHUCK JOHNSON DESIGNERS: CHUCK JOHNSON, KEN KOESTER
DESIGN FIRM/CLIENT: BRAINSTORM, INC. COUNTRY: USA
■ (OPPOSITE) ART DIRECTOR: SHIGEO KATSUOKA DESIGNERS: SHIGEO KATSUOKA, AKIKO SHIMAZU
CLIENT: TSUKAMOTO CO., LTD. COUNTRY: JAPAN

GRAPHIS PUBLICATIONS

GRAPHIS, THE INTERNATIONAL BI-MONTHLY JOURNAL OF VISUAL COMMUNICATION
GRAPHIS SHOPPING BAG, AN INTERNATIONAL COLLECTION OF SHOPPING BAG DESIGN
GRAPHIS MUSIC CD, AN INTERNATIONAL COLLECTION OF CD DESIGN
GRAPHIS BOOK DESIGN, AN INTERNATIONAL COLLECTION OF BOOK DESIGN
GRAPHIS DESIGN, THE INTERNATIONAL ANNUAL OF DESIGN AND ILLUSTRATION
GRAPHIS STUDENT DESIGN, THE INTERNATIONAL ANNUAL OF DESIGN AND COMMUNICATION BY STUDENTS
GRAPHIS ADVERTISING, THE INTERNATIONAL ANNUAL OF ADVERTISING
GRAPHIS BROCHURES, A COMPILATION OF BROCHURE DESIGN
GRAPHIS PHOTO, THE INTERNATIONAL ANNUAL OF PHOTOGRAPHY
GRAPHIS ALTERNATIVE PHOTOGRAPHY, THE INTERNATIONAL ANNUAL OF ALTERNATIVE PHOTOGRAPHY
GRAPHIS NUDES, A COLLECTION OF CAREFULLY SELECTED SOPHISTICATED IMAGES
GRAPHIS POSTER, THE INTERNATIONAL ANNUAL OF POSTER ART
GRAPHIS PACKAGING, AN INTERNATIONAL COMPILATION OF PACKAGING DESIGN
GRAPHIS LETTERHEAD, AN INTERNATIONAL COMPILATION OF LETTERHEAD DESIGN
GRAPHIS DIAGRAM, THE GRAPHIC VISUALIZATION OF ABSTRACT, TECHNICAL AND STATISTICAL FACTS AND FUNCTIONS
GRAPHIS LOGO, AN INTERNATIONAL COMPILATION OF LOGOS
GRAPHIS EPHEMERA, AN INTERNATIONAL COLLECTION OF PROMOTIONAL ART
GRAPHIS PUBLICATION, AN INTERNATIONAL SURVEY OF THE BEST IN MAGAZINE DESIGN
GRAPHIS ANNUAL REPORTS, AN INTERNATIONAL COMPILATION OF THE BEST DESIGNED ANNUAL REPORTS
GRAPHIS CORPORATE IDENTITY, AN INTERNATIONAL COMPILATION OF THE BEST IN CI DESIGN
GRAPHIS TYPOGRAPHY, AN INTERNATIONAL COMPILATION OF THE BEST IN TYPOGRAPHIC DESIGN

GRAPHIS PUBLIKATIONEN

GRAPHIS, DIE INTERNATIONALE ZWEIMONATSZEITSCHRIFT DER VISUELLEN KOMMUNIKATION
GRAPHIS SHOPPING BAG, TRAGTASCHEN-DESIGN IM INTERNATIONALEN ÜBERBLICK
GRAPHIS MUSIC CD, CD-DESIGN IM INTERNATIONALEN ÜBERBLICK
GRAPHIS BOOKS, BUCHGESTALTUNG IM INTERNATIONALEN ÜBERBLICK
GRAPHIS DESIGN, DAS INTERNATIONALE JAHRBUCH ÜBER DESIGN UND ILLUSTRATION
GRAPHIS STUDENT DESIGN, DAS INTERNATIONALE JAHRBUCH ÜBER KOMMUNIKATIONSDESIGN VON STUDENTEN
GRAPHIS ADVERTISING, DAS INTERNATIONALE JAHRBUCH DER WERBUNG
GRAPHIS BROCHURES, BROSCHÜRENDESIGN IM INTERNATIONAL ÜBERBLICK
GRAPHIS PHOTO, DAS INTERNATIONALE JAHRBUCH DER PHOTOGRAPHIE
GRAPHIS ALTERNATIVE PHOTOGRAPHY, DAS INTERNATIONALE JAHRBUCH ÜBER ALTERNATIVE PHOTOGRAPHIE
GRAPHIS NUDES, EINE SAMMLUNG SORGFÄLTIG AUSGEWÄHLTER AKTPHOTOGRAPHIE
GRAPHIS POSTER, DAS INTERNATIONALE JAHRBUCH DER PLAKATKUNST
GRAPHIS PACKAGING, EIN INTERNATIONALER ÜBERBLICK ÜBER DIE PACKUNGSGESTALTUNG
GRAPHIS LETTERHEAD, EIN INTERNATIONALER ÜBERBLICK ÜBER BRIEFPAPIERGESTALTUNG
GRAPHIS DIAGRAM, DIE GRAPHISCHE DARSTELLUNG ABSTRAKTER TECHNISCHER UND STATISTISCHER DATEN
GRAPHIS LOGO, EINE INTERNATIONALE AUSWAHL VON FIRMEN-LOGOS
GRAPHIS EPHEMERA, EINE INTERNATIONALE SAMMLUNG GRAPHISCHER DOKUMENTE DES TÄGLICHEN LEBENS
GRAPHIS MAGAZINDESIGN, EINE INTERNATIONALE ZUSAMMENSTELLUNG DES BESTEN ZEITSCHRIFTEN-DESIGNS
GRAPHIS ANNUAL REPORTS, EIN INTERNATIONALER ÜBERBLICK ÜBER DIE GESTALTUNG VON JAHRESBERICHTEN
GRAPHIS CORPORATE IDENTITY, EINE INTERNATIONALE AUSWAHL DES BESTEN CORPORATE IDENTITY DESIGNS
GRAPHIS TYPOGRAPHY, EINE INTERNATIONALE ZUSAMMENSTELLUNG DES BESTEN TYPOGRAPHIE DESIGN

PUBLICATIONS GRAPHIS

GRAPHIS, LA REVUE BIMESTRIELLE INTERNATIONALE DE LA COMMUNICATION VISUELLE
GRAPHIS SHOPPING BAG, UNE COMPILATION INTERNATIONALE SUR LE DESIGN DES SACS À COMMISSIONS
GRAPHIS MUSIC CD, UNE COMPILATION INTERNATIONALE SUR LE DESIGN DES CD
GRAPHIS BOOKS, UNE COMPILATION INTERNATIONALE SUR LE DESIGN DES LIVRES
GRAPHIS DESIGN, LE RÉPERTOIRE INTERNATIONAL DE LA COMMUNICATION VISUELLE
GRAPHIS STUDENT DESIGN, UN RÉPERTOIRE INTERNATIONAL DE PROJTS D'EXPRESSION VISUELLE D'ÉDUTIANTS
GRAPHIS ADVERTISING, LE RÉPERTOIRE INTERNATIONAL DE LA PUBLICITÉ
GRAPHIS BROCHURES, UNE COMPILATION INTERNATIONALE SUR LE DESIGN DES BROCHURES
GRAPHIS PHOTO, LE RÉPERTOIRE INTERNATIONAL DE LA PHOTOGRAPHIE
GRAPHIS ALTERNATIVE PHOTOGRAPHY, LE RÉPERTOIRE INTERNATIONAL DE LA PHOTOGRAPHIE ALTERNATIVE
GRAPHIS NUDES, UN FLORILÈGE DE LA PHOTOGRAPHIE DE NUS
GRAPHIS POSTER, LE RÉPERTOIRE INTERNATIONAL DE L'AFFICHE
GRAPHIS PACKAGING, LE RÉPERTOIRE INTERNATIONAL DE LA CRÉATION D'EMBALLAGES
GRAPHIS LETTERHEAD, LE RÉPERTOIRE INTERNATIONAL DU DESIGN DE PAPIER À LETTRES
GRAPHIS DIAGRAM, LE RÉPERTOIRE GRAPHIQUE DE FAITS ET DONNÉES ABSTRAITS, TECHNIQUES ET STATISTIQUES
GRAPHIS LOGO, LE RÉPERTOIRE INTERNATIONAL DU LOGO
GRAPHIS EPHEMERA, LE GRAPHISME – UN ÉTAT D'ESPRIT AU QUOTIDIEN
GRAPHIS PUBLICATION, LE RÉPERTOIRE INTERNATIONAL DU DESIGN DE PÉRIODIQUES
GRAPHIS ANNUAL REPORTS, PANORAMA INTERNATIONAL DU MEILLEUR DESIGN DE RAPPORTS ANNUELS
GRAPHIS CORPORATE IDENTITY, PANORAMA INTERNATIONAL DU MEILLEUR DESIGN D'IDENTITÉ CORPORATE
GRAPHIS TYPOGRAPHY, LE RÉPERTOIRE INTERNATIONAL DU MEILLEUR DESIGN DE TYPOGRAPHIE

PUBLICATION NO. 262 (ISBN 1-888001-02-X)
© COPYRIGHT UNDER UNIVERSAL COPYRIGHT CONVENTION
COPYRIGHT © 1996 BY GRAPHIS PRESS CORP., DUFOURSTRASSE 107, 8008 ZURICH, SWITZERLAND
JACKET AND BOOK DESIGN COPYRIGHT © 1996 BY PEDERSEN DESIGN
141 LEXINGTON AVENUE, NEW YORK, N.Y. 10016 USA

PRINTED IN HONG KONG BY PARAMOUNT PRINTING COMPANY LIMITED

COMMENTARIES

KOMMENTARE

COMMENTAIRES

Scott Mednick

Logos, symbols, logotypes, identities, graphic identifiers, icons, trademarks, service marks—what does it all mean? □ Back in 1976, I was designing logos. I know it may sound like ancient history, but I actually had clients paying me to create symbols to adorn stationery and business cards. Although, now that I think of it, one of my first clients was a lawyer and I can't recall if I ever got paid... □ Also in 1976, the United States of America unleashed the bicentennial logo upon the general public. The appearance of this symbol, created by Chermayeff and Geismar, marked the first time I became aware of a logo that wasn't designed for a specific company (I had not yet realized at that point that our country *is* a company). No mere symbol for an annual report, this logo appeared on hats, coffee mugs, banners, license plate holders—you name it. The first major shot had been fired in the merchandising war. Movie studios and athletic leagues must have been paying attention. □ From that point on, logos seemed to change forever and multiply. It might have been a gradual change, but as I sit here twenty years later, the reasons for a logo's existence have changed completely. When a logo was truly a corporate symbol, I had the opportunity to design dozens of marks for fine corporations. These marks subsequently adorned office papers and reception area walls with representations of corporate values. Occasionally, I was thrilled to see the marks I had created appear on a uniform or vehicle. In those days, consistency was the key. The challenge was to nail down a corporate identity program and prescribe—through use of a manual— the rules, the laws, the Ten Commandments of Logodom. Life and logos were simpler then. □ Today, logos are fashion statements. MTV is the standard bearer and companies want to address their audience with a logo which suggests they are hip. When designing a logo, I always begin by considering the specific criteria for that company. Sometime in the early eighties, the word "hip" began to creep into many clients' criteria. Since I strived to design symbols to last at least twenty years, would these symbols always be hip and contemporary? From my perspective, I was doomed to fail. Finally I realized my perspective needed adjustment. □ Today I am more likely to be designing logos to appear on hats, t-shirts, and jackets than on letterheads. Clients' symbols have become fashion statements. They have become messages whose medium has been altered forever. □ In the crowded world of cyberspace, there are icons for the grabbing. Everywhere you turn, symbols confront us. But now, as never before, the personality embodied by the mark itself has superseded that mark's communication of a company's function. It used to be that when designing a logo for a bakery, one would rely on traditional symbols and letterforms to create a new representation of one, the other, or both. Creating an effective logo is more difficult in an economy in which the

SCOTT MEDNICK, FOUNDER OF THE MEDNICK GROUP, HAS PRODUCED A VARIETY OF MARKETING MATERIALS FROM PACKAGING TO LOGOS FOR MAJOR INTERNATIONAL CORPORATIONS AS WELL AS MANY PROFESSIONAL SPORTS TEAMS. HIS WORK FREQUENTLY APPEARS IN MAJOR DESIGN PUBLICATIONS AND HE HAS WON MANY NATIONAL AND INTERNATIONAL AWARDS. HIS WORK IS REPRESENTED IN THE PERMANENT COLLECTION OF THE LIBRARY OF CONGRESS AS WELL AS NUMEROUS MUSEUMS.

product is actually a service or an intellectual commodity. The baker's hat no longer serves as a point of departure. □ As awareness of the service sector increases, what it does may become less important than how it does it. Personality: that's the ticket! □ Who's to say that a symbol can really project a company's image anyway? I contend that the success of the fat check mark that symbolizes the Nike phenomenon has less to do with that symbol and what it projects than with the fact that it triggers memories of all the spectacular work done by Nike's graphic design team, headed by Ron Dumas, and of the brilliant advertising imagery created by Wieden and Kennedy. The Swoosh—great symbol or great campaign? I suggest that the logo is not the end-all-and-be-all of the system. Usage has become the key. □ The rules are no longer so rigid. Multiple color variations, alternate formats, even multiple symbols are applied. The old rules, it seems, do not apply to the contemporary corporation or its audience. □ In 1990 when I reworked much of CBS's graphic look, I was haunted by the image of Lou Dorfsman waving a disappointing finger at me. The great CBS eye had been a standard by which identity programs were measured, but I was breaking all the old rules and assigning new graphic realities to this venerable symbol. I am sure pastel colors and playing with the proportions of the typeface were not what Lou would have had in mind. But the "Tiffany" network had never anticipated the ignominy of being the first major network (of the three big networks) to fall from first place to a dismal third in one season. My job was to help fix that. □ In reworking the print look—from affiliates to national advertising—we managed what seemed impossible. The network looked and felt younger from graphics to advertising to programming. The team of which I am proud to have been a part produced the equally unlikely "Worst to First" season as the network regained its ratings crown. The logo functioned as a marketing tool. Audiences have changed. So have their graphic worlds. Sorry, Lou. □ This brings me back to that attorney. While I don't recall any remuneration, I do know it was not my last experience with lawyers and logos. I have often wondered how many new logos are in my head waiting to be designed. Well, the lawyers may answer this for me. □ Last year, my company designed the identity systems for several new Time Warner companies. In one of the symbols we used a three-dimensional sphere with a highlight in the upper left quadrant. Time Warner attorneys later called to inform me that 3M's lawyers claimed that 3M had already trademarked that sphere and highlight. These attorneys say that by using the sphere in its logo, Time Warner may be in violation of 3M's trademark protection. The lawyers wanted to know if I had seen or copied the aforementioned sphere. I found it funny until I realized they were serious about trademarking the sphere. □ Logos, symbols, logotypes, identities, graphic identifiers, icons, trademarks, service marks—what does it all mean? Maybe it just means more lawyers. ■

Logos, Symbole, Schriftzüge, Identitäten, graphische Kennzeichen, Ikonen, Markenzeichen für Produkte und Dienstleistungen. Was bedeutet das alles? Vielleicht bedeutet
es, dass jeder diese Dinge jetzt zu schätzen weiss und deshalb auch ihre Schöpfer
schätzt. □ Im Jahre 1976 habe ich noch Logos entworfen. Ehrlich. Ich weiss, es klingt
nach vergangenen Zeiten, aber ich hatte Kunden, die mich für den Entwurf eines
Markenzeichens bezahlten. Symbole, die ihr Briefpapier und ihre Visitenkarten zieren
sollten. Einer meiner ersten Kunden war übrigens ein Anwalt. Ich kann mich nicht
erinnern, ob er mich je bezahlt hat.... □ Ebenfalls im Jahre 1976 konfrontierten die USA
die eher unbeleckten Massen mit dem Logo für die Zweihundertjahrfeier. Das von
Chermayeff und Geismar kreierte Symbol war das erste Logo für mich, das nicht für
eine Firma entworfen worden war. (Zumindest hatte ich zu jener Zeit noch nicht
realisiert, dass unser Land in der Tat eine Firma ist.) Das Logo war nicht einfach ein
Symbol für einen Jahresbericht, ich sah es auf Hüten, Kaffeetassen, Fahnen, Autos,
praktisch überall. Genau genommen, kann ich mich nicht erinnern, in jenem Jahr
irgend etwas anderes gesehen zu haben. Der erste bedeutende Schuss im Merchan-
dising-Krieg war gefallen. Filmstudios und Sportclubs müssen sehr genau hingeschaut
haben. □ Von da an schienen Logos sich ständig zu verändern. Und zu vermehren. Das
mag nach und nach passiert sein, aber jetzt, 20 Jahre später, dürften die Gründe für
die Existenz eines Logos völlig andere sein. □ Als das Logo noch ein echtes Firmen-
symbol war, hatte ich Gelegenheit, einige Dutzend für sehr gute Firmen zu entwerfen,
die ihre Briefschaften und die Wände ihrer Empfangsräume mit diesen Interpretationen
ihrer Firmenkultur schmückten. Manchmal konnte ich die Logos, die ich entworfen
hatte, sogar auf einer Uniform oder einem Auto bewundern. □ Damals war Kontinuität
das Zauberwort. Es galt, das Identitäts-Programm für die Firmen zu definieren und die
Anwendungsregeln in einem Handbuch festzulegen. Das waren die Gesetze. Die zehn
Gebote der Logokultur. □ Leben und Logos waren damals unkomplizierter. Aber alles
hat sich verändert. Eines Tages wurden Logos zu modischen Aussagen, und MTV
spielte dabei den Leithammel. Die Firmen wollten das Publikum mit ihren Logos zu
verstehen geben, dass sie, die Firmen, voll durchsteigen – also hip sind. □ Wenn ich
ein Logo entwerfe, beginne ich immer mit den besonderen Kriterien für eine Firma.
Irgendwann in den achziger Jahren schlich sich in diese Kriterien auf der Kundenseite
das Wort hip ein. Da ich hoffte, Logos zu entwerfen, die mindestens 20 Jahre bestehen
würden, stellte sich die Frage, wie es hip und dabei zeitlos bleiben konnte. Aus meiner
Sicht hatte ich überhaupt keine Chance. Bis ich begriff, dass meine Perspektive einer
Korrektur bedurfte. □ Wenn ich heute ein Logo entwerfe, wird es mit grösster Wahr-

. . . .
SCOTT MEDNICK GRÜNDETE THE MEDNICK GROUP MIT BÜROS IN LOS ANGELES UND ATLANTA UND
HAT EINE VIELZAHL VON MARKETING-INSTRUMENTEN VON VERPACKUNGEN BIS ZU LOGOS FÜR BE-
DEUTENDE INTERNATIONALE FIRMEN UND SPORT-TEAMS PRODUZIERT. SEINE ARBEITEN WERDEN
IMMER WIEDER IN WICHTIGEN FACHZEITSCHRIFTEN GEZEIGT UND SIE WURDEN MIT VIELEN NATIO-
NALEN UND INTERNATIONALEN PREISEN AUSGEZEICHNET. SEINE ARBEITEN SIND IN DEN SAMMLUN-
GEN DER LIBRARY OF CONGRESS UND ZAHLREICHER MUSEEN VERTRETEN. MEDNICK IST IM VOR-
STAND VIELER UMWELTORGANISATIONEN UND UNTERSTÜTZT AUSBILDUNGSPROGRAMME FÜR KINDER.

scheinlichkeit auf Hüten, T-Shirts und Jacken erscheinen und nicht auf Briefpapier. Das Medium für diese besonderen Botschaften der Firmen hat sich ein für alle Mal verändert. □ Und in der Welt des Cyberspace wimmelt es von Ikonen. Wohin man sich wendet, immer scheint es eine Art von Symbolik zu geben. Aber heute, und das hat es nie gegeben, ist die Funktion des Markenzeichens als Ausdruck einer Firma überholt, viel wichtiger ist seine eigene Persönlichkeit. □ Wenn man seinerzeit z.B. ein Logo für eine Bäckerei entwarf, konnte man auf bewährte traditonelle Symbole und Schriftarten zurückgreifen, auf das eigene Talent, um aus dem einen oder anderen oder beiden etwas Neues zu machen. □ In einer von Dienstleistungen geprägten Wirtschaft, in welcher die Produkte der Auftraggeber eben Dienstleistungen oder intellektuelle Güter sind, wird es schwieriger, sich auszudrücken – mit der Mütze des Bäckers war das einfacher. □ Und während der Dienstleistungssektor immer mehr ins Zentrum der Aufmerksamkeit seiner potentiellen Clientèle gerät, wird womöglich das, was eine Firma tut, weniger wichtig als die Art, wie sie es tut. Persönlichkeit – das ist das Zauberwort. □ Wer kann eigentlich behaupten, dass ein Symbol tatsächlich das Image einer Firma zum Ausdruck bringen kann. Ich behaupte, dass der schwungvolle, kräftige Haken, der zum Symbol des Nike-Phänomens wurde, weniger mit dem Symbol und seiner Aussage zu tun hat als mit der Tatsache, dass dieses Symbol zum Auslöser von Erinnerungen an all die spektakulären Arbeiten des von Ron Dumas geleiteten Nike-Graphik-Design-Teams und die brillante Nike-Werbung von Wieden und Kennedy ist. Ein grossartiges Symbol oder eine grossartige Kampagne? Ich würde sagen, dass das Logo nicht alles ist. Auf den Einsatz kommt es an. □ Die Regeln sind längst nicht mehr so streng. Zahlreiche Farbvariationen, verschiedene Formate und sogar mehrere Symbole sind möglich. Es scheint, dass die alten Regeln nicht mehr zu den heutigen Firmen und ihrem Publikum passen. □ Als ich 1990 den graphischen Auftritt von CBS überarbeitete, sah ich im Geiste Lou Dorfsman vor mir, der enttäuscht abwinkte. Das grossartige CBS-Auge war der Masstab, an dem visuelle Identitätsprogramme gemessen wurden. Und nun war ich dabei, sämtliche alten Regeln zu brechen und für alle Niederlassungen um Lande neue (graphische) Realitäten zu schaffen. Ich bin sicher, dass Lou nicht daran gedacht hatte, Pastell-Farben einzusetzen oder mit den Proportionen der Schrift zu experimentieren. Aber der Sender hatte sich nie träumen lassen, dass er in nur einer Saison vom ersten auf den schändlichen dritten – sprich letzten – Platz unter den drei grössten Sendern fallen könnte. Und ich sollte helfen, das wieder in Ordnung zu bringen. □ Durch die Überarbeitung des Auftritts in gedruckter Form – von internen Drucksachen bis zur landesweiten Werbung – gelang uns das scheinbar Unmögliche. Von der Graphik über die Werbung bis zu den Programmen wirkte der Sender jünger. Und das Team, bei dem ich mitarbeiten durfte, schaffte das ebenfalls scheinbar Unmögliche: Einschaltquoten, die CBS vom letzten auf den ersten Platz beförderten. Das Logo als Marketing-Instrument. Das Publikum hat sich verändert und sein Geschmack auch. Sorry, Lou. □ Das bringt mich wieder auf den Anwalt. Wenn ich mich auch nicht an mein Honorar erinnern kann, so weiss ich doch, dass dies nicht meine letzte Erfahrung mit Anwälten und Logos geblieben ist. Ich habe mich gefragt, wie viele neue Logos ich im Kopf habe. Nun, die Anwälte mögen das für mich beantworten. □ Letztes Jahr hat meine Firma Identitäts-Programme für mehrere neue Firmen von Time Warner entworfen. Bei einem der Symbole verwenden wir einen dreidimensional wirkenden Planeten – mit Lichteinfall oben links. Die Anwälte von Time Warner riefen mich letzte Woche an, um mir mitzuteilen, dass die Anwälte von 3M diesen Planeten mit eben diesem Highlight als ihre Marke geschützt haben und sie, Time Warner's Anwälte, darauf aufmerksam machen, dass Time Warner mit diesem Planeten als Teil des Logos 3Ms Markenrechte verletzen könnte. Die Anwälte wollten wissen, ob ich den erwähnten Planeten gesehen bzw. kopiert habe. Das war ziemlich komisch, bis mir klar wurde, dass sie ernsthaft davon sprachen, dass jemand einen Planeten schützen kann. □ Logos, Symbole, Schriftzüge, Identitäten, graphische Kennzeichen, Ikonen, Markenzeichen für Produkte und Dienstleistungen. Was bedeutet das alles? Vielleicht einfach noch mehr Anwälte. ■

....

Logos, symboles, logotypes, identités, signalisation graphique, icônes, marque de fabriques pour les produits et les services. Qu'est-ce que signifie tout cela? Peut-être que cela signifie que chacun d'entre nous a appris à apprécier tous ces éléments visuels, et, par conséquent, le métier de graphiste. □ En 1976, je créais encore des logos. Cela peut sembler de l'histoire ancienne, mais j'avais effectivement des clients qui me payaient pour créer des logos qui allaient orner leur papier à lettres ou leurs cartes de visite. Je me rappelle qu'un de mes premiers clients était un avocat. En revanche, je ne me souviens pas si j'avais été payé. □ C'est également en 1976 que les Etats-Unis d'Amérique ont lancé le logo du Bicentenaire auprès d'un public plutôt inculte. Le logo créé à cette occasion par Chermayeff et Geismar était le premier, à ma connaissance, qui n'ait pas été créé pour une entreprise. Sans doute n'avais-je pas encore compris que notre pays est en réalité une gigantesque entreprise. Le logo était omniprésent. Je l'ai vu sur des chapeaux, des tasses, des drapeaux, des voitures, bref partout. Je crois bien que c'est la seule chose que j'ai remarquée cette année-là. Un

....

SCOTT MEDNICK EST LE FONDATEUR DU MEDNICK GROUP, DONT LES BUREAUX SE TROUVENT À LOS ANGELES ET À ATLANTA. IL A CRÉÉ UNE GRANDE VARIÉTÉ DE PRODUITS DE MARKETING, DES EMBALLAGES AUX LOGOS, ET CECI POUR PLUSIEURS ENTREPRISES INTERNATIONALES AINSI QUE DE NOMBREUX CLUBS SPORTIFS. SES TRAVAUX SONT FRÉQUEMMENT PUBLIÉS DANS DES MAGAZINES DE DESIGN ET ONT ÉTÉ RÉCOMPENSÉS PAR DE NOMBREUSES DISTINCTIONS NATIONALES ET INTERNATIONALES. SES RÉALISATIONS FIGURENT ÉGALEMENT DANS LA COLLECTION PERMANENTE DE LA LIBRARY OF CONGRESS ET DANS DE NOMBREUX MUSÉES. IL EST MEMBRE DE PLUSIEURS ORGANISATIONS ÉCOLOGIQUES ET PARTICIPE À DES PROGRAMMES ÉDUCATIFS POUR ENFANTS.

premier bastion était tombé dans la guerre du merchandising. Les clubs sportifs et les studios de cinéma auront sans doute été les premiers à le remarquer. □ A partir de ce moment-là, les logos se sont multipliés et diversifiés à l'infini. C'est arrivé graduellement, mais aujourd'hui – vingt ans plus tard – les raisons qui justifient l'existence d'un logo ont totalement changé. □ A l'époque où le logo symbolisait encore l'entreprise, j'ai eu l'occasion d'en créer une douzaine pour de très bonnes sociétés. Ils trônaient sur leur papier à lettres et dans leur salle de réception et étaient l'expression de leur culture d'entreprise. De temps à autre, j'avais le plaisir de voir les logos que j'avais créés apparaître sur un uniforme ou sur une voiture. □ En ce temps-là, la continuité était le maître mot. Il s'agissait de définir une fois pour toutes un programme d'identité institutionnelle et de s'y tenir. Il y avait des lois et on obéissait sans broncher aux dix commandements de la création de logos. □ La vie et les logos étaient plus simples. Mais tout cela a changé depuis. Les logos sont devenus des emblèmes à la mode, et MTV fait figure d'étalon de référence. Dès lors, les entreprises ont voulu se présenter à leur public avec des logos accrocheurs, dans le vent et dans le ton. □ Lorsque je crée un logo, je commence toujours avec des critères spécifiques se rapportant à l'entreprise. Durant les années quatre-vingt, la question de mode a commencé à faire partie des critères d'évaluation des clients. Etant donné que mon objectif était de créer des logos qui aient une durée de vie d'au moins 20 ans, la question se posait pour moi de savoir comment faire en sorte que mon logo ne vieillisse pas. De mon point de vue, je n'avais aucune chance de m'en sortir. Mais j'ai réalisé que je devais revoir ma position. □ Aujourd'hui, lorsque je crée un logo, il y a toutes les chances pour qu'il figure sur des chapeaux, des T-shirts et des vestes et non sur un papier à en-tête. Les logos font dorénavant partie de la mode et les supports ont radicalement changé. □ Le Cyberspace grouille litté-ralement d'icônes. Où que l'on regarde, il y a partout des symboles. Mais ce qui est nouveau aujourd'hui, c'est que le logo possède une personnalité indépendamment de l'entreprise qu'il symbolise. □ Lorsqu'on créait jadis un logo pour une boulangerie, on pouvait se référer à une imagerie et à des caractères traditionnels, et compter sur son talent personnel pour créer une nouvelle identité à partir de ces éléments. □ En revanche, dans une économie axée principalement sur les services, il devient beaucoup plus difficile de communiquer une identité que lorsqu'il s'agit de représenter un bonnet de boulanger. □ Aujourd'hui, à l'heure où les prestations de services revêtent une importance croissante aux yeux des clients potentiels, la façon de faire d'une entrepreise a sans doute plus d'impact sur ces derniers que sa production effective. □ J'estime que le symbole de Nike, le fameux petit «crochet», n'a pas contribué au succès de l'entreprise parce qu'il véhicule un message particulier, mais plutôt parce qu'il fait revivre des images, il se place dans une continuité et entraîne des associations: on se souvient des travaux spectaculaires de l'équipe des designers graphiques de Nike, placée sous la férule de Ron Dumas, ou encore des publicités détonantes de Wieden et Kennedy. Un très bon logo ou une fabuleuse campagne? Je dirais que le logo n'est pas tout, tout dépend l'emploi qu'on en fait. □ Les règles sont de moins en moins rigides. Il existe de nombreuses variations de couleurs, des formats très variés et un réservoir de symboles inépuisable. Il semble simplement que les anciennes règles ne conviennent plus aux clients actuels et au public en général. □ En 1990, lorsque j'ai retravaillé l'image graphique de CBS, j'étais hanté par l'idée de Lou Dorfsman pointant vers moi un doigt désapprobateur. Le gros œil de CBS était l'étalon de mesure de toute identité institutionnelle de la chaîne. Or là, j'étais en train de briser toutes les règles et de créer à partir de ce vénérable symbole une nouvelle réalité graphique pour toutes les sociétés affiliées du pays. Je suis sûr qu'introduire des tons pastels et jouer sur les proportions des caractères n'était pas ce que Lou Dorfsman avait en tête. Mais le réseau CBS n'avait jamais imaginé qu'il pouvait, en l'espace d'une saison, passer de la première à la troisième place parmi les trois grandes chaînes de télévision. Mon rôle était de contribuer à renverser cette tendance. □ En rafraîchissant le graphisme de tous les imprimés – de la documentation interne jusqu'à la publicité internationale – nous avons réussi à gagner un pari qui semblait impossible. La chaîne, de la promotion jusqu'aux programmes, donnait l'impression d'avoir subi une véritable cure de jouvence. Et l'équipe avec laquelle j'avais eu le plaisir de travailler a elle aussi réalisé l'impossible: le taux d'audience augmentait à nouveau et CBS retrouvait sa place en tête du peloton. Le logo est un instrument de marketing. Et le goût du public a changé. Désolé Lou. □ L'an dernier, mon agence a créé des programmes d'identité institutionnelle pour diverses filiales du groupe Time Warner. Pour l'un de ces logos, j'ai utilisé une sphère tridimensionnelle avec un faisceau de lumière placé dans le quart supérieur gauche. Les avocats de Time Warner m'ont téléphoné pour m'informer que les avocats de 3M les avaient contactés, leur disant que Time Warner risquait d'être poursuivie en justice pour violation de la loi sur la protection des marques, le logo sphérique de 3M faisant précisément l'objet d'une protection. Les avocats voulaient savoir si j'avais vu ou copié la sphère en question. C'était comique, jusqu'au moment où j'ai compris qu'ils étaient sérieux et qu'une sphère pouvait bel et bien faire l'objet d'une protection de marque. □ Logos, symboles, logotypes, identités, signalisation graphique, icônes, marques de fabrique pour les produits et les services. Qu'est-ce que cela signifie? Peut-être simplement plus de travail pour les avocats. ■

PAUL IBOU

Good design is more than a particular style; it is an attitude toward an intrinsic quality. It is why people react against things which are vulgar, fake, or unimportant and are drawn to things which have guts, wit, and ingenuity. If this sounds more like a moral than an aesthetic attitude, that is how it should be—good design affects more than just the eye. □ Design is essentially the fruit of thought and hard work. In today's mass market, every consumer can be a design critic. The more discriminating people become, the more manufacturers will have to realize that merchandise must meet the demands we place on it—good design will have to be a fundamental part of any successful business. □ A corporate design should neither be linked nor limited to a specific culture, but understood worldwide by people of different cultural backgrounds. Design (logos and corporate designs) should be independent of most standards and accessible to anyone, regardless of education or intelligence. To maintain its value or prestige, both of which are of vital importance, design must always meet functional and aesthetic requirements—based on uniform rules of the principles of design, the same way language is based on grammar. □ In recent years these principles have changed very little despite the influence of computers and the cybernetical wave. However, designers have learned quite a lot through experience, including how to conceptualize and simplify. The essence of finding an adequate way of introducing a logo design concept to the public has remained the same. In fact, creating logos and corporate identities still ranks among the most rewarding and challenging activities in the field of creativity. Graphic designers are among the most influential architects of a better world. They deserve more recognition from the highest ranks of the economical, social, and cultural sector.

MAKING THEIR MARKS

□ The logo symbol created for a company or organization is intended to ease visual perception. The simpler the form of the logo, the more effectively it catches the human eye.

□ A logo should neither be linked nor limited to a specific culture or style, but should be understood worldwide by people of varying cultural backgrounds.

□ A logo should be independent of any educational standard and accessible to anyone, regardless of education or intelligence.

□ The design of a logo should be based on uniform rules of the art of design, in the same way language is based on grammar.

PAUL IBOU STARTED HIS CAREER IN 1961 IN ANTWERPEN AS A FREELANCE DESIGNER, CONCENTRATING ON LOGO DESIGN, CORPORATE IDENTITY PROGRAMS, AND BOOK DESIGN. IN COOPERATION WITH INTERECHO PRESS HE HAS PUBLISHED NUMEROUS DESIGN AND ART BOOKS. IN 1985 HE INITIATED THE INTERNATIONAL LOGO CENTER (ILC) WHERE THE FIRST WORLD SYMBOL FESTIVAL TOOK PLACE FOR THE FIRST TIME IN 1994 AND WILL BE HELD EVERY OTHER YEAR. PAUL IBOU IS A MEMBER OF MANY DESIGN ASSOCIATIONS AND A FREQUENT GUEST SPEAKER AND JURY MEMBER IN CONTESTS. HE HAS EXHIBITED HIS DESIGN WORK AS WELL AS HIS CONSTRUCTIVE ART ALL OVER THE WORLD.

☐ Essentially a logo is the fruit of thought and hard work. In order not to lose its value and prestige, which are of vital importance, the logo must always meet functional and aesthetic application requirements.

☐ In thirty years of logo design, very little has changed, although experience teaches a lot, including conceptualizing and simplifying.

☐ Creating logos and corporate identities rank among the most rewarding but also the most challenging activities of graphic design.

☐ There will always be a link between current trends, society and design, due to the international exchange of communication and media. The influence of computer design and new cybernetical support cannot be ignored in the field of logo design.

Gutes Design ist mehr als nur ein bestimmter Stil, es ist eine Haltung, die der Qualität verpflichtet ist. Die Menschen sträuben sich gegen Dinge, die für sie «nicht stimmen», die vulgär oder einfach unwichtig sind. Dagegen fühlen sie sich von Dingen angezogen, die Intelligenz und Witz verraten, von Dingen, die «stimmen». Wenn das eher nach Moral als nach einer ästhetischen Haltung klingt, so ist das beabsichtigt: Gutes Design beeinflusst mehr als nur das Auge, und es ist die Frucht von Überlegungen und harter Arbeit. ☐ In unserem heutigen Massenmarkt kann jeder Konsument zum Design-Kritiker werden. Je kritischer die Menschen werden, desto mehr werden die Hersteller sich bemühen müssen, den Anforderungen gerecht zu werden – und gutes Design wird zweifellos eine Grundvoraussetzung für ein erfolgreiches Unternehmen sein. ☐ Das Erscheinungsbild einer Firma sollte nie auf ein spezifisches kulturelles Umfeld ausgerichtet oder auf dieses beschränkt sein, es sollte von Menschen aus ganz verschiedenen Kulturen weltweit verstanden werden können. Design, d.h. Logos und Erscheinungsbilder, sollten für jedermann zugänglich sein, unabhängig von der Ausbildung oder Intelligenz. Um seinen Wert oder sein Prestige zu erhalten, beides wesentliche Faktoren, muss Design unter allen Umständen ästhetischen und funktionalen Anforderungen gerecht werden und sich dabei an allgemeingültige Regeln der Gestaltung halten, so wie eine Sprache sich an die Grammatik hält. ☐ In den letzten Jahren hat sich nur wenig verändert, abgesehen vom Einfluss der neuen Technologien. Nach wie vor geht es darum, dass ein Designer dank seiner Erfahrung gelernt hat, konzeptuell zu denken und zu vereinfachen. Im Grunde sind die Voraussetzungen für die erfolgreiche Einführung eines Logos und seine Akzeptanz beim Publikum die gleichen geblieben. ☐ Corporate Identity Design, einschliesslich der Gestaltung von Logos, gehört noch immer zu den grössten und dankbarsten kreativen Heraus-

PAUL IBOU BEGANN SEINE KARRIERE ALS GRAPHIK-DESIGNER 1961 IN ANTWERPEN. ZU SEINEN SPEZIALGEBIETEN GEHÖREN DIE GESTALTUNG VON LOGOS UND UMFASSENDE C.I. PROGRAMME SOWIE BUCHGESTALTUNG. SEIT 1974 HAT ER ZUSAMMEN MIT INTERECHO PRESS ZAHLREICHE DESIGN -UND KUNSTBÜCHER HERAUSGEGEBEN. VOR ZEHN JAHREN GRÜNDETE ER DAS INTERNATIONALE LOGO CENTER (ITC), WO 1994 ZUM ERSTEN MAL DAS WORLD SYMBOL FESTIVAL STATTFAND, DAS ALS BIENNALE GEPLANT IST. PAUL IBOU IST MITGLIED ZAHLREICHER DESIGN-VERBÄNDE, GEFRAGTER GASTREFERENT UND JUROR BEI INTERNATIONALEN WETTBEWERBEN. SEINE DESIGN-ARBEITEN SOWIE AUCH SEINE ARBEITEN ALS KONSTRUKTIVER KÜNSTLER WURDEN IN ALLER WELT AUSGESTELLT.

forderungen für den Graphik-Designer, der zu den wichtigsten Architekten einer besseren Welt gehört. Graphik-Designer verdienen die Anerkennung von höchster Stelle in wirtschaftlichen, sozialen und kulturellen Bereichen.

ZEICHEN SETZEN – IN KÜRZE

· ·

☐ Ein Logo, das für eine Firma oder Organisation entworfen wird, hat die Aufgabe, die optische Wahrnehmung zu erleichtern. Je einfacher die Form eines Logos, desto nachhaltiger wird es auf das Auge wirken.

☐ Ein Logo sollte weder an eine spezifische Kultur gebunden noch auf sie beschränkt sein, und es sollte für alle Menschen, unabhängig von ihrer Kultur, verständlich sein.

☐ Ein Logo sollte unabhängig von der Bildung oder Intelligenz des Betrachters für jedermann zugänglich sein.

☐ Das Design von Logos sollte auf den Grundregeln der Gestaltung aufbauen, so wie eine Sprache auf eine Grammatik aufbaut.

☐ Ein Logo ist im Wesentlichen das Ergebnis von Überlegungen und harter Arbeit. Um bestehen zu können, um seinen Wert und sein Prestige zu erhalten, muss ein Logo den funktionalen und ästhetischen Anforderungen seiner Bestimmung gerecht werden.

☐ In der Gestaltung von Logos hat sich wenig verändert, auch wenn Erfahrung eine Menge lehrt, wie konzeptuelles Denken und Reduzierung.

☐ Die Schaffung von Logos, von Corporate Identity Design, gehört zu den dankbarsten, aber auch schwierigsten Aufgaben des Graphik-Designers.

☐ Es wird immer eine Verbindung zwischen den aktuellen Trends, der Gesellschaft und dem Design geben, was dem internationalen Gedankenaustausch und den neuen Medien zu verdanken ist. Der Einfluss der durch den Computer gegebenen neuen Möglichkeiten können im Bereich des Logo-Designs nicht vernachlässigt werden.

· ·

Un bon design ne se résume pas à un style ; c'est le produit d'une philosophie fondée sur la recherche de la qualité. C'est pourquoi l'on éprouve instinctivement une réaction de rejet à l'égard des choses laides, vulgaires ou banales, alors que les choses belles – qui marient l'esprit, l'intelligence, l'authenticité – nous séduisent d'emblée. Si ces propos s'apparentent plus à une attitude morale qu'à une démarche esthétique, tant mieux. Car un bon design va au-delà de la forme. Un bon design est le fruit d'une réflexion approfondie, d'un travail assidu. ☐ Dans notre société de production et de consommation de masse, chacun peut se poser en «critique de design». Or, plus les consommateurs seront critiques, plus les fabricants devront tenir compte de leurs exigences. Le design deviendra alors un élément essentiel, dont dépendra le succès

· ·

PAUL IBOU A DÉBUTÉ SA CARRIÈRE À ANVERS EN TANT QUE GRAPHISTE INDÉPENDANT, CONCENTRANT SES ACTIVITÉS SUR LA CRÉATION DE LOGOS ET L'ÉLABORATION D'IMPORTANTS PROGRAMMES DE CORPORATE IDENTITY AINSI QUE LA CONCEPTION GRAPHIQUE DE DIFFÉRENTS OUVRAGES. DEPUIS 1974, IL A ÉDITÉ, EN COLLABORATION D'INTERECHO PRESS, DE NOMBREUX LIVRES D'ART ET DE GRAPHISME. IL Y A DIX ANS, IL A FONDÉ L'ITC (INTERNATIONAL LOGO CENTER) OÙ S'EST TENU POUR LA PREMIÈRE FOIS EN 1994 LE WORLD SYMBOL FESTIVAL QUI AURA LIEU TOUS LES DEUX ANS. PAUL IBOU EST TRÈS RECHERCHÉ POUR SES TALENTS DE CONFÉRENCIER LORS DE CONCOURS INTERNATIONAUX À L'OCCASION DESQUELS IL ENDOSSE À SES HEURES LE RÔLE DE JURÉ.

d'une entreprise. □ L'identité visuelle d'une entreprise ne doit pas se limiter à un espace culturel particulier, mais, au contraire, se jouer des frontières culturelles et géographiques. Logos ou tout autre élément de corporate design doivent ainsi se distinguer par leur «universalité» qui les rend accessibles à chaque être humain, indépendamment de son éducation ou de son intelligence. Pour conserver sa valeur et son prestige – facteurs essentiels –, le design doit concilier esthétique et fonctionnalité, en respectant pour ce faire des règles strictes, tout comme le langage est régi par la grammaire. □ Les dernières années n'ont pas apporté de changements notoires, hormis le développement de la cybernétique et de la CAO. L'expérience a toutefois permis aux designers d'évoluer vers des formes plus simples, plus épurées. Mais les paramètres déterminant la qualité d'un logo et son impact sur le public demeurent inchangés. □ En termes de créativité, la conception de logos ou d'autres éléments de corporate design reste le défi le plus passionnant à relever pour les designers, nouveaux démiurges d'un monde meilleur... Le rôle fondamental qui est le leur mérite ainsi d'être reconnu à sa juste valeur dans les plus hautes sphères de la vie économique, sociale et culturelle.

RÉSUMÉ DES POINTS ESSENTIELS
....

□ Un logo – qu'il soit créé pour une société ou une organisation – doit être identifiable au premier coup d'œil. Plus il est simple, plus l'impact visuel est fort.

□ Un logo ne doit pas se limiter à un espace culturel particulier, mais doit, au contraire, se jouer des frontières culturelles et géographiques.

□ Un logo doit se distinguer par son «universalité» qui le rend accessible à chaque être humain, indépendamment de son éducation ou de son intelligence.

□ Le design d'un logo doit répondre à des règles strictes, tout comme le langage est régi par la grammaire.

□ Un logo réussi est le fruit d'une réflexion approfondie, d'un travail assidu. Pour conserver sa valeur et son prestige – facteurs essentiels —, un logo doit concilier esthétique et fonctionnalité.

□ Au cours des trente dernières années, la création de logos n'a pas connu de profonds changements. L'expérience a toutefois permis aux designers d'évoluer vers des formes plus simples, plus épurées.

□ En termes de créativité, la conception de logos reste le défi le plus passionnant à relever.

□ Il y aura toujours un lien entre les modes et tendances, la société et le design grâce à l'internationalisation des moyens de communication et aux nouveaux médias. L'influence croissante de la CAO et de la cybernétique sur la création de logos ne peut être ignorée.

GRAPHIS LOGO 3

HAS BEEN PRODUCED IN CONJUNCTION WITH
THE "STRATHMORE PRESENTS GRAPHIS" LOGO EXHIBITION
AND THROUGH THE GENEROUS SUPPORT OF
STRATHMORE PAPER.

GRAPHIS LOGO 3

WURDE MIT FREUNDLICHER UNTERSTÜTZUNG VON
STRATHMORE PAPER UND IN VERBINDUNG MIT DER AUSSTELLUNG
«STRATHMORE PRESENTS GRAPHIS»
PRODUZIERT.

GRAPHIS LOGO 3

A ÉTÉ PRODUIT EN COOPERATION AVEC
L'EXPOSITION INTITULÉE «STRATHMORE PRESENTS GRAPHIS»
ET GRÂCE AU SOUTIEN GÉNÉREUX DE
STRATHMORE PAPER.

1

2

3

5

1 CLIENT: MELTZER & MARTIN DESIGN FIRM: SULLIVANPERKINS ART DIRECTOR/DESIGNER: ANDREA PETERSON COUNTRY: USA INDUSTRY/PURPOSE: PUBLIC RELATIONS – RELATIONS PUBLIQUES ■ 2 CLIENT: STUBENRAUCH & SIMON DESIGN FIRM: FACTOR DESIGN ART DIRECTOR/DESIGNER/ILLUSTRATOR: RÜDIGER GÖTZ COUNTRY: GERMANY INDUSTRY: ADVERTISING AGENCY – WERBEAGENTUR – AGENCE DE PUBLICITÉ ■ 3 CLIENT: CHALLENGE PROMOTIONS DESIGN FIRM: PINKHAUS DESIGN CORP. ART DIRECTORS: JOEL FULLER, TODD HOUSER DESIGNER/ILLUSTRATOR: TODD HOUSER COUNTRY: USA INDUSTRY/PURPOSE: PUBLIC RELATIONS, ADVERTISING PROMOTIONS – PUBLIC RELATIONS UND WERBEPROMOTIONEN – RELATIONS PUBLIQUES ET PROMOTIONS

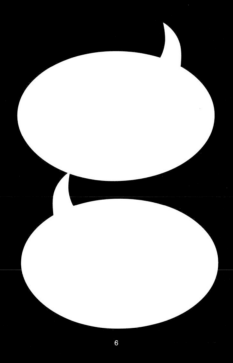

6

PUBLICITAIRES ■ 4 CLIENT: WIERMAN FEED CO. DESIGN FIRM: BASLER DESIGN GROUP ART DIRECTOR: BILL BASLER DESIGNERS: BILL BASLER, COLLEEN WENDLING COUNTRY: USA INDUSTRY/PURPOSE: FEED MANUFACTUR- ER – FUTTERHERSTELLER – PRODUCTEUR DE FOURRAGE ■ 5 CLIENT: BBDO DESIGN FIRM: MIRES DESIGN, INC. ART DIRECTOR/DESIGNER: JOSÉ SERRANO ILLUSTRATOR: TRACY SABIN COUNTRY: USA INDUSTRY/PURPOSE: ADVERTISING AGENCY – WERBEAGENTUR – AGENCE DE PUBLICITÉ ■ 6 CLIENT: GROUP GALLAGHER DESIGN FIRM: JOSEPH RATTAN DESIGN ART DIRECTOR: JOSEPH RATTAN DESIGNERS: GREG MORGAN, JOSEPH RATTAN ILLUSTRATOR: DIANA MCKNIGHT COUNTRY: USA INDUSTRY/PURPOSE: PUBLIC RELATIONS – RELATIONS PUBLIQUES

1 CLIENT/DESIGN FIRM: THE LEONHARDT GROUP DESIGNERS/ILLUSTRATORS: JEFF WELSH, JON CANNELL COUNTRY: USA INDUSTRY/PURPOSE: MULTIMEDIA ■ 2 CLIENT: FRANKFURTER BAUMSCHULEN DESIGN FIRM: GIRAFFE WERBE-AGENTUR DESIGNER: LOTHAR TANZYNA COUNTRY: GERMANY INDUSTRY/PURPOSE: TREE NURSERY, HORTICULTURE – BAUMSCHULE, GARTENBAUBETRIEB – PÉPINIÈRE ET HORTICULTURE ■ 3 CLIENT: GREEN BY NATURE DESIGN FIRM: THE SILENT PARTNERS ART DIRECTOR: BLAINE LIFTON DESIGNER/ILLUSTRATOR: MICHAEL SCHWAB COUNTRY: USA INDUSTRY/PURPOSE: GARDENING SUPPLY STORE – LADEN FÜR GARTENGERÄTE – MAGASIN D'OUTILS DE JARDINAGE ■ 4 CLIENT: THE HOKUREN FEDERATION OF AGRICULTURAL CO-OPERATIVE ASSOCIATION DESIGN

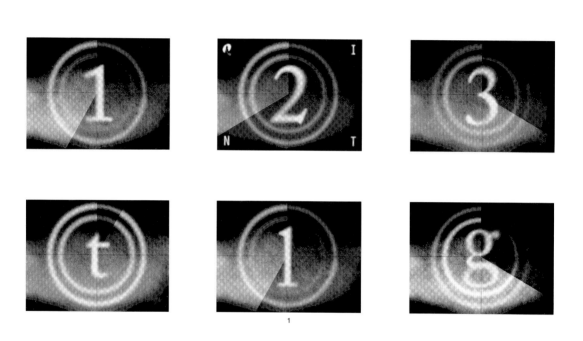

1

FIRM: SHIGEO KATSUOKA DESIGN STUDIO ART DIRECTOR: SHIGEO KATSUOKA DESIGNERS: SHIGEO KATSUOKA, KATSU YOSHIDA COUNTRY: JAPAN INDUSTRY/PURPOSE: AGRICULTURAL ASSOCIATION – LANDWIRTSCHAFT-LICHER VERBAND – ASSOCIATION D'AGRICULTEURS ■ 5 CLIENT: WOODS EQUIPMENT COMPANY DESIGN FIRM: MUELLER BAKER ASSOCIATES ART DIRECTOR: KRISTI MUELLER DESIGNER: KRISTI MUELLER COUNTRY: USA INDUSTRY: FARM EQUIPMENT MANUFACTURER – HERSTELLER VON LANDWIRTSCHAFTLICHEN MASCHINEN – FABRICANT DE MACHINES AGRICOLES ■ 6 CLIENT: PERUTNINA PTUJ ART DIRECTOR: EDI BERK DESIGNER: EDI BERK COUNTRY: SLOVENIA INDUSTRY/PURPOSE: POULTRY FARM – HÜHNERFARM – ELEVAGE DE POULES

2

3

4

WOODS

5

6

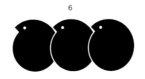

1 CLIENT: MAHLUM & NORDFORS MCKINLEY GORDON DESIGN FIRM: HORNALL ANDERSON DESIGN WORKS, INC. ART DIRECTOR: JACK ANDERSON DESIGNERS: JACK ANDERSON, LEO RAYMUNDO, SCOTT EGGERS COUNTRY: USA INDUSTRY: ARCHITECTURAL FIRM – ARCHITEKTURBÜRO – BUREAU D'ARCHITECTES ■ **2** CLIENT/DESIGN FIRM: KROG ART DIRECTOR/DESIGNER: EDI BERK COUNTRY: SLOVENIA INDUSTRY/PURPOSE: STUDIO FOR ARCHITECTURE

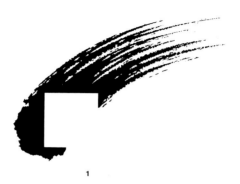

1

2

3

AND GRAPHIC DESIGN – ARCHITEKTUR- UND DESIGNATELIER – BUREAU D'ARCHITECTES ET DE DESIGN ■ **3** CLIENT: TORCHIA DESIGN FIRM: LISKA AND ASSOCIATES ART DIRECTOR: STEVE LISKA DESIGNER: NANCY BLACKWELL COUNTRY: USA INDUSTRY/PURPOSE: ARCHITECTURAL FIRM – ARCHITEKTURBÜRO – BUREAU D'ARCHITECTES ■ **4** CLIENT: Q. INK DESIGN FIRM: BRAINSTORM, INC. ART DIRECTOR/DESIGNER/ILLUSTRATOR: KEN KOESTER COUNTRY: USA INDUSTRY/PURPOSE: ARTISTS' REPRESENTATIVE – KÜNSTLERAGENTUR – AGENCE D'ARTISTES

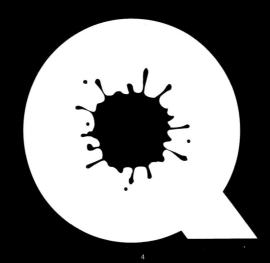

4

1 CLIENT: AVEX.D.D. DESIGN FIRM: ROUND TABLE ASSOC. ART DIRECTOR: HIDEHISA SASAKI DESIGNER: HIDEHISA SASAKI COUNTRY: JAPAN DESCRIPTION:TECHNO LABEL ■ **2** CLIENT: COPELAND REIS AGENCY DESIGN FIRM: MIRES DESIGN ART DIRECTOR/DESIGNER: JOHN BALL COUNTRY: USA DESCRIPTION:TALENT AGENCY – KÜNSTLER-AGENTUR – AGENCE D'ARTISTES ■ **3** CLIENT: JANEART DESIGN FIRM: HIXO, INC. ART DIRECTOR: MIKE HICKS DESIGNER: MATT HECK COUNTRY: USA DESCRIPTION:ARTISTS' REPRESENTATIVE – KUNSTAGENTUR – AGENCE D'ART ■ **4** CLIENT: MAIN STREET GARAGE DESIGN FIRM: MULLER + COMPANY ART DIRECTOR: JOHN MULLER DESIGNER: ANGELA COLEMAN COUNTRY: USA INDUSTRY: GARAGE FOR VINTAGE RACE CARS – WERKSTATT FÜR ALTE RENNWAGEN – GARAGE POUR VOITURES DE COLLECTION ■ **5** CLIENT: BECKLEY IMPORTS DESIGN FIRM:

1

2

3

SAYLES GRAPHIC DESIGN ART DIRECTOR/DESIGNER: JOHN SAYLES ILLUSTRATOR: JOHN SAYLES COUNTRY: USA DESCRIPTION:IMPORT CAR SERVICE SHOP – WERKSTATT FÜR IMPORTWAGEN – GARAGE POUR VOITURES D'IM-PORTATION ■ **6** CLIENT: DELTA SIERRA DESIGN FIRM: BRIGHT & ASSOCIATES DESIGNER: KONRAD BRIGHT COUNTRY: USA DESCRIPTION:RACE CAR DRIVER – RENNFAHRER – COUREUR AUTOMOBILE ■ **7** CLIENT: CHIAT DAY DESIGN FIRM: CHARLES S. ANDERSON DESIGN COMPANY ART DIRECTOR: CHARLES S. ANDERSON DESIGNERS: CHARLES S. ANDERSON, TODD PIPER-HAUSWIRTH COUNTRY: USA DESCRIPTION:CAR MANUFACTURER – AUTOHERSTELLER – CONSTRUCTEUR AUTOMOBILE ■ **8** CLIENT: FÖVAROSI AUTO PIAC DESIGN FIRM: ART FORCE STUDIO ART DIRECTOR: ATTILA SIMON DESIGNER: ATTILA SIMON ILLUSTRATORS: ATTILA SIMON, CSABA ALMASSY COUNTRY: HUNGARY DESCRIPTION:AUTOMOTIVE DEALER – AUTOHÄNDLER – CONCESSIONNAIRE EN AUTOMOBILES.

4

5

6

7

8

1

2

3

4

5

BEAUTY · BEAUTÉ

1 CLIENT: ACIS, INC. DESIGN FIRM: NAYLOR, DEDONATO & WOLF ART DIRECTOR/DESIGNER: BILL HEALEY ILLUSTRATOR: CHRIS MCROBBIE COUNTRY: USA INDUSTRY/PURPOSE: SKIN CARE PRODUCTS BASED ON THE GINGKO LEAF – HAUTPFLEGEMITTEL AUF GINGKO-BASIS – PRODUITS COSMÉTIQUES AU GINGKO ■ **2, 6** CLIENT/DESIGN FIRM: MATRIX ESSENTIALS, INC. CREATIVE DIRECTOR: DENNIS LUBIN (6) ART DIRECTOR/DESIGNER: SUSAN TATE COUNTRY: USA INDUSTRY: HAIRCARE AND BEAUTY PRODUCTS FOR FULL SERVICE SALONS – HAARPFLEGE- UND KOSMETIKPRODUKTE FÜR FULL-SERVICE-SALONS – PRODUITS COSMÉTIQUES POUR INSTITUTS DE BEAUTÉ ■ **3** CLIENT: BOW WOW BARBER DESIGN FIRM: SIBLEY/PETEET DESIGN, INC. ART

6

DIRECTOR: DEREK WELCH DESIGNER: DEREK WELCH ILLUSTRATOR: DEREK WELCH COUNTRY: USA BUSINESS: BARBER – FRISEUR – COIFFEUR ■ **4** CLIENT: ICE GODDESS PERFUMES DESIGN FIRM: KEVIN AKERS DESIGN ART DIRECTOR: KEVIN AKERS DESIGNER: KEVIN AKERS ILLUSTRATOR: KEVIN AKERS COUNTRY: USA INDUSTRY: WOMEN'S COSMETIC LINE – KOSMETIKLINIE FÜR FRAUEN – LIGNE DE PRODUITS COSMÉTIQUES POUR FEMMES ■ **5** CLIENT: SALON LA COUR DESIGN FIRM: GARY ALFREDSON DESIGN DESIGNER: GARY ALFREDSON COUNTRY: USA BUSINESS: UPSCALE HAIR SALON – GEHOBENER COIFFEUR-SALON – SALON DE COIFFURE HAUT DE GAMME

1

2

3

4

1 Client: Aurora: Expressions of Alaska Design Firm: Cronan Design, Inc. Art Director: Michael Cronan Designer: Michael Cronan Illustrator: Michael Cronan Country: USA Industry/Purpose: Catalog Company – Verlag – Maison d'édition info. ■ **2** Client: Subaru Committee Design Firm: Keizo Matsui & Associates Art Director/Designer: Keizo Matsui Country: Japan Industry/Purpose: Automotive – Automobil – Automobile ■ **3** Client: Commcor, Inc. Design Firm: Naylor, Dedonato & Wolf Art Director: Bill Healey Designer: Bill Healey Illustrator: Bill Healey Country: USA Industry:

5

Management Holding Company ■ **4** Client: Christiansen, Fritsch, Giersdorf, Grant & Sperry Design Firm: Hornall Anderson Design Works, Inc. Art Director: Jack Anderson Designers: Jack Anderson, David Bates Country: USA Industry/Purpose: Marketing Communications ■ **5** Client: Marketing Vision Design Firm: Joseph Rattan Design Art Director: Joseph Rattan Designer: Diana McKnight Country: USA Industry/Purpose: Strategic Marketing and Product Development – Marketing-Strategien und Produktentwicklung – Conseil en marketing et développement de produits

1

$$\begin{bmatrix} \text{WORLDWIDE} \\ \text{OPERATIONS} \end{bmatrix}$$

2

$$\begin{bmatrix} \text{MISSION} \\ \text{STATEMENT} \end{bmatrix}$$

3

$$\begin{bmatrix} \text{STRATEGIC} \\ \text{INITIATIVES} \end{bmatrix}$$

4

$$\begin{bmatrix} \text{VALUES} \end{bmatrix}$$

5

$$\begin{bmatrix} \text{ARCHITECTURAL} \\ \text{DIRECTION} \end{bmatrix}$$

6

$$\begin{bmatrix} \text{COMPONENTS} \end{bmatrix}$$

7

8

1 CLIENT: XACTDATA CORPORATION DESIGN FIRM: HORNALL ANDERSON DESIGN WORKS, INC. ART DIRECTOR: JACK ANDERSON DESIGNERS: JACK ANDERSON, LISA CERVENY, JANA WILSON, JULIE KEENAN COUNTRY: USA INDUSTRY: DISTRIBUTIVE SYSTEM BACK-UP – BACK-UP-SYSTEME – SYSTÈMES BACK-UP ■ **2–7** CLIENT: SUN MICROSYSTEMS, INC. DESIGN FIRM: EARL GEE DESIGN ART DIRECTOR/ILLUSTRATOR: EARL GEE DESIGNERS: EARL GEE, FANI CHUNG COUNTRY: USA INDUSTRY: WORLDWIDE OPERATIONS PROGRAM OF A COMPUTER WORKSTATION MANUFACTURER – WELTWEITES BETRIEBSPROGRAMM EINES HERSTELLERS

9

VON COMPUTER-ARBEITSSTATIONEN – SYSTÈME D'EXPLOITATION INTERNATIONAL D'UN FABRICANT DE STATIONS DE TRAVAIL INFORMATISÉES ■ **8** CLIENT: CONCIERGE SOFTWARE COMPANY DESIGN FIRM: STUDIO D DESIGN ART DIRECTOR: LAURIE DEMARTINO DESIGNER: ILLUSTRATOR: LAURIE DEMARTINO COUNTRY: USA INDUSTRY: SOFTWARE MANUFACTURER – SOFTWARE-HERSTELLER – FABRICANT DE LOGICIELS ■ **9** CLIENT: SILICON GRAPHICS DESIGN FIRM: CRONAN DESIGN, INC. ART DIRECTOR/DESIGNER/ILLUSTRATOR: MICHAEL CRONAN COUNTRY: USA INDUSTRY: COMPUTER COMPANY – COMPUTER-FIRMA – SOCIÉTÉ D'INFORMATIQUE

1 Client: LIANT, INC. Design Firm: HIXO, INC. Art Director: MIKE HICKS Designers: TOM POTH, MIKE HICKS Country: USA Industry: COMPUTER SOFTWARE – LOGICIELS ■ 2 Client: INTERACTIVE PLANET, INC. Design Firm: MELIA DESIGN GROUP Designer: TODD SIMMONS Country: USA Industry: DESKTOP PROGRAMMERS – DESKTOP-PROGRAMMIERER – DÉVELOPPEMENT DE LOGICIELS DESKTOP ■ 3 Client: MIDCOM COMMUNICATIONS Design Firm: HORNALL ANDERSON DESIGN WORKS, INC. Art Director: JOHN HORNALL Designers: JOHN HORNALL, JANA NISHI, DAVID BATES Country: USA Industry: TELEPHONE SERVICE RESELLER – WIEDERVERKÄUFER VON TELEPHONDIENSTEN ■ 4 Client: PLANET CRAFTERS, INC. Design Firm: CREATIVE R+D Art Director/Designer/Illustrator: PHIL SCOPP Country: USA Industry: COMPUTER SOFT-WARE – LOGICIELS ■ 5 Client: RALF BÄUMENER COMPUTERTECHNIK Design Firm: MARKUS HEINBACH Art Director: MARKUS HEINBACH Designer: MARKUS HEINBACH Country: GERMANY Industry: COMPUTER TECH-NIC – COMPUTERTECHNIK ■ 6 Client: PALLADIUM Design Firm: CLEMENT MOK DESIGNS Art Director: MARK CRUMPACKER Designer: GREGG HEARD Project Manager: KAREN ROEHL-SIVAK Country: USA Industry: PRODUCER OF CD-ROMS FOR CHILDREN – HERSTELLER VON CD ROMS FÜR KINDER – FABRICANT DE CD ROMS POUR ENFANTS ■ 7 Client: RTJ MEDICAL SOFTWARE CORP. Design Firm: CREATIVE R+D Art Director: PHIL SCOPP Designer: PHIL SCOPP Illustrator: PHIL SCOPP Country: USA Industry: MEDICAL SOFTWARE – SOFTWARE FÜR MEDIZINISCHE ZWECKE – LOGICIELS POUR APPLICATIONS MÉDICALES ■ 8 Client: GUIDANCE TECHNOLOGIES Design Firm: NAYLOR, DEDONATO & WOLF Art Director/Designer: BILL HEALEY Illustrator:

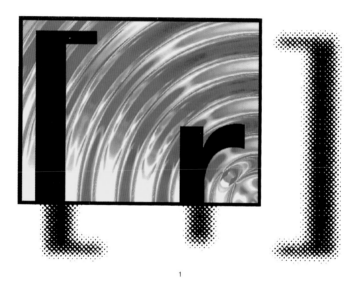

1

JIM PROKELL Country: USA Industry: SOFTWARE MANUFACTURING AND RESEARCH – SOFTWARE-HERSTEL-LUNG UND -FORSCHUNG – FABRICATION DE LOGICIELS ET RECHERCHE ■ 9 Client: INQUISITION SOFTWARE CORPORATION Design Firm: SAYLES GRAPHIC DESIGN Art Director/Designer/Illustrator: JOHN SAYLES Country: USA Industry: SOFTWARE DEVELOPER – SOFTWARE-ENTWICKLUNG – DÉVELOPPEMENT DE LOGI-CIELS ■ 10 Client: STAC ELECTRONICS Design Firm: MIRES DESIGN, INC. Art Director/Designer: JOHN BALL Country: USA Industry: ELECTRONICS – ELEKTRONIK – ÉLECTRONIQUE ■ 11 Client: FRAME TECHNOLOGY Design Firm: MICHAEL PATRICK PARTNERS Art Direction/Design: MICHAEL PATRICK PARTNERS Country: USA Industry: DOCUMENT PROCESSING SOFTWARE – SOFTWARE-ENTWICKLUNG – DÉVELOPPEMENT DE LOGI-CIELS ■ 12 Client: CHISELVISION Design Firm: ROTH+ASSOCIATES Art Director: WAYNE C. ROTH Designer: PETER DE SIBOUR Country: USA Industry: ELECTRONIC IMAGING – ELEKTRONISCHE BILDHERSTELLUNG – INFOGRAPHIE ■ 13 Client: DIGITAL ARTS Design Firm: DESIGN/ART, INC. Art Director/Designer: NORMAN MOORE Country: USA Industry: COMPUTER 3D ANIMATION SOFTWARE – SOFTWARE FÜR 3D-ANIMATION – LOGICIELS D'ANIMATION TRIDIMENSIONNELLE ■ 14 Client: ELLIPSIS Design Firm: KORN DESIGN Art Director/Designer: DENISE KORN Country: USA Industry: COMPUTER SOFTWARE – LOGICIELS ■ 15 Client: ELSEWARE CORP. Design Firm: HORNALL ANDERSON DESIGN WORKS, INC. Art Director: JACK ANDERSON Designers: JACK ANDERSON, DEBRA HAMPTON, LEO RAYMUNDO Country: USA Industry: SOFTWARE DEVEL-OPER, SPECIALIZING IN FONT MANIPULATION – ENTWICKLUNG VON SOFTWARE FÜR COMPUTERSCHRIFTEN – FABRICANT DE LOGICIELS SPÉCIALISÉ DANS LES POLICES DE CARACTÈRES ■ 16 Client: NET INFOR-MATION SYSTEMS, INC. Design Firm: THE LEONHARDT GROUP Designers: JON CANNELL, JEFF WELSH Country: USA Industry: COMPUTER SPECIALISTS – COMPUTER-SPEZIALISTEN – SPÉCIALISTES INFORMATIQUES

2

3

4

5

PALLADIUM
INTERACTIVE

6

7

8

9

10

11

12

13

14

15

16

1

AIRDATA

2

3

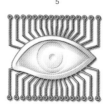

4

5

1 Client: GCC INC. Design Firm: SHIGEO KATSUOKA DESIGN STUDIO Art Director: SHIGEO KATSUOKA Designers: SHIGEO KATSUOKA, HIRONOBU YAMADA Country: JAPAN Industry/Purpose: INFORMATION PROCESSING SERVICE COMPANY – DATENVERARBEITUNGSFIRMA – SOCIÉTÉ DE TRAITEMENT DE DONNÉES ■ **2** Client: MCCAW CELLULAR COMMUNICATIONS, INC. Design Firm: TIM GIRVIN DESIGN, INC. Art Director: TIM GIRVIN Designer: GRAINNE CARVIL Country: USA Industry/Purpose: CELLULAR TECHNOLOGY PRODUCTS – PRODUKTE DER ZELLULAR-TECHNOLOGIE – PRODUITS DE LA TECHNOLOGIE CELLULAIRE ■ **3** Client: MINDSCAPE Design Firm: THE MEDNICK GROUP Art Director: SCOTT MEDNICK Designers: SCOTT MEDNICK, TOM THORNTON Illustrator: TOM THORNTON Country: USA Industry/Purpose: CD ROM CONTENT PROVIDER

6

– CD ROM PRODUKTIONEN ■ **4** Client: NET IMAGES Design Firm: THE DESIGN OFFICE OF WONG & YEO Art Directors: VALERIE WONG, HOCK WAH YEO Designers: HOCK WAH YEO, VALERIE WONG, EKO TJOEK Country: USA Industry/Purpose: MARKETING ON THE COMPUTER WORLDWIDE WEB – MARKETING IM WELTWEITEN COMPUTER WEB – MARKETING PAR LE WORLD WIDE WEB (WWW) ■ **5** Client: OCP COMMUNICATE Design Firm: DESIGN AHEAD Designer: RALF STUMPF Country: GERMANY Industry/Purpose: SOFTWARE AND HARDWARE DEVELOPMENT AND CONSULTING – SOFTWARE UND HARDWARE, BERATUNG UND ENTWICKLUNG ■ **6** Client: ISSC Design Firm: PAGANUCCI DESIGN, INC. Art Director/Designer: BOB PAGANUCCI Country: USA Industry: INFORMATION TECHNOLOGY – INFORMATIONSTECHNOLOGIE – TECHNOLOGIE D'INFORMATION

1 CLIENT: TECHNICOLOR DESIGN FIRM: LANDOR ASSOCIATES CREATIVE DIRECTOR: COURTNEY REESER ART DIRECTOR: LINDON GRAY LEADER DESIGNER: MICHAEL COLLINS, VIRGINIA VOVCHUK COUNTRY: USA INDUSTRY: HIGH TECH, ENTERTAINMENT – HIGH TECH, UNTERHALTUNG – HIGH-TECH DIVERTISSEMENTS ■ 2 CLIENT: SYSTEM BUILDER DESIGN FIRM: HARCUS DESIGN ART DIRECTOR: ANNETTE HARCUS DESIGNER/ILLUSTRATOR: MARIO MILOSTIC COUNTRY: AUSTRALIA INDUSTRY: COMPUTER SOFTWARE PROGRAMS – COMPUTER-SOFTWARE – LOGICIELS ■ 3 CLIENT: X TECHNOLOGY, INC. DESIGN FIRM: SHEAFF DORMAN PURINS ART DIRECTOR/DESIGNER: ULDIS PURINS COUNTRY: USA INDUSTRY: SOFTWARE DEVELOPER – SOFTWARE-ENTWICKLER – DÉVELOPPEMENT DE LOGICIELS ■ 4 CLIENT: SQL SYSTEMS DESIGN FIRM: KILTER INCORPORATED ART DIRECTOR: TIM SCHUMANN DESIGNER: TIM SCHUMANN COUNTRY: USA INDUSTRY: SOFTWARE DEVELOPER FOR

1

2

3

MAINTENANCE – SOFTWARE-ENTWICKLUNG FÜR WARTUNGSAUFGABEN – FABRICANT DE LOGICIELS DE MAIN-TENANCE ■ 5 CLIENT: TRASHER GRAPHICS DESIGN FIRM: POLLARD DESIGN ART DIRECTOR/DESIGNER: JEFF POLLARD COUNTRY: USA INDUSTRY: COMPUTER GRAPHICS – COMPUTER-GRAPHIK – INFOGRAPHIE ■ 6 CLIENT: VALUE INTEGRATED NETWORK, INC. DESIGN FIRM: PETRICK DESIGN ART DIRECTOR: ROBERT PETRICK DESIGNER: MICHAEL GOLEC COUNTRY: USA INDUSTRY: COMPUTER SOFTWARE PROGRAMMING – PROGRAMMIE-RUNG VON COMPUTER-SOFTWARE – PROGRAMMATION DE LOGICIELS ■ 7 CLIENT: AHA! SOFTWARE ART DIRECTOR: DAVID CURTIS DESIGNER: DAVID CURTIS COUNTRY: USA INDUSTRY: SOFTWARE – LOGICIELS ■ 8 CLIENT: FRITZEN & PARTNER EDV ORGANISATION DESIGN FIRM: DESIGN AHEAD DESIGNER: RALF STUMPF COUNTRY: GERMANY INDUSTRY: ELECTRONIC DATA ORGANISATION – EDV ORGANISATION – ORGANISATION TED

4

5

6

aha

7

8

1

2

3

4

5

1 Client: Silicon Graphics Design Firm: Cronan Design, Inc. Art Director/Designer/Illustrator: Michael Cronan Country: USA Industry/Purpose: Computer – Ordinateurs ■ **2** Client: The 3DO Co. Design Firm: Mark Anderson Design Art Director: Mark Anderson Designers: Greg Heard, Mark Anderson Country: USA Industry/Purpose: Software – Logiciels ■ **3** Client: Evans & Sutherland Design Firm: Clarkson Creative Art Director/Designer/Illustrator: Larry Clarkson Country: USA Industry/Purpose: Graphics Simulation – Graphische Computersimulation – Logiciels de Simulation Graphique ■ **4** Client: Rendition Design Firm: Mortensen Design Art Director/Designer: Gordon

6

MORTENSEN Country: USA Industry/Purpose: 3-D Rendering and High Speed Animation for the PC – 3D-Darstellungen und Animationen für PCS – Applications et Animations Tridimenionnelles pour Micro-Ordinateurs ■ **5** Client: Silicon Graphics Design Firm: Cronan Design, Inc. Art Director: Michael Cronan Designers: Michael Cronan, Lisa van Zandt, Anthony Yell Illustrators: Michael Cronan, Anthony Yell Country: USA Industry/Purpose: Computer – Ordinateurs ■ **6** Client: Computer Repair Design Firm: S.D. Zyne Art Director/Designer: Spencer Walters Country: USA Industry: Computer Repair – Computer-Reparaturservice – Service de Réparation d'Ordinateurs

1

2

3

4

1, 2 CLIENT: AG DESIGN FIRM: FACTOR DESIGN ART DIRECTOR/DESIGNER/ILLUSTRATOR: RÜDIGER GÖTZ COUNTRY: GERMANY INDUSTRY: ARCHITECTURAL FIRM — ARCHITEKTURBÜRO — BUREAU D'ARCHITECTES ■ 3 CLIENT: TERRA-NOVA CONSTRUCTION DESIGN FIRM: BRIGHT & ASSOCIATES DESIGNER: KONRAD BRIGHT COUNTRY: USA INDUSTRY: CONSTRUCTION — BAUWIRTSCHAFT — ENTREPRISE DE CONSTRUCTION ■ 4 CLIENT: ALL PRO WALLPAPER DESIGN

5

FIRM: MIRES DESIGN ART DIRECTOR/DESIGNER/ILLUSTRATOR: JOSÉ SERRANO COUNTRY: USA INDUSTRY: WALLPAPER INSTALLATION AND REMOVAL — TAPEZIERER — SOCIÉTÉ SPÉCIALISÉE DANS LA TAPISSERIE ■ 5 CLIENT: HAGE CONSTRUCTION DESIGN FIRM: THORBURN DESIGN ART DIRECTOR: BILL THORBURN DESIGNER: CHAD HAGEN COUNTRY: USA INDUSTRY/PURPOSE: CONSTRUCTION — BAUWIRTSCHAFT — ENTREPRISE DE CONSTRUCTION

1

2

3

4

5

1 Client: DAVID & GOLIATH BUILDERS, INC. Design Firm: CI DESIGN Art Director/Designer: JIM TAUGHER Country: USA Industry: CONSTRUCTION – BAUWIRTSCHAFT – ENTREPRISE DE CONSTRUCTION ■ 2 Client: TIMBERFORM BUILDERS Design Firm: SWIETER DESIGN UNITED STATES Art Director/Designer: JOHN SWIETER Country: USA Industry: TIMBER-FRAME CONSTRUCTION ■ 3 Client: H + M ELECTRIC Design Firm: KIRBY STEPHENS DESIGN, INC. Art Director/Designer: KIRBY STEPHENS Country: USA Industry: INDUSTRIAL ELECTRICAL CONTRACTOR – ELEKTRIKER FÜR INDUSTRIEANLAGEN – SYSTÈMES ÉLECTRIQUES

6

INDUSTRIELS ■ 4 Client: MESSERLI + VOGEL Design Firm: SCARTON SGD Art Director: BRUNO SCARTON Designer: BRUNO SCARTON Country: SWITZERLAND Industry/Purpose: ENGINEERING – INGENIEURBÜRO – INGÉNIEURS-CONSEIL ■ 5 Client: MARKUS HINTZEN Design Firm: FACTOR DESIGN Art Director/Designer/ Illustrator: RÜDIGER GÖTZ Country: GERMANY Industry/Purpose: ELEVATORS – AUFZUGKONZEPT – ÉLÉ-VATATEURS ■ 6 Client: BASA Design Firm: KROG Art Director/Designer: EDI BERK Country: SLOVENIA Industry: ARRANGEMENT SERVICES – DIENSTLEISTUNGSBETRIEB – ENTREPRISE DE PRESTATIONS DE SERVICES

1 CLIENT: HUMAN RESOURCES MANAGEMENT DESIGN FIRM/ART DIRECTOR/DESIGNER/ILLUSTRATOR: KLAUS FRANKE COUNTRY: GERMANY INDUSTRY/PURPOSE: PERSONNEL AND CONVENTION MANAGEMENT – PERSONAL- UND KON-GRESSMANAGEMENT – MANAGEMENT DES RESSOURCES HUMAINES ET ORGANISATION DE CONGRÈS ■ 2 CLIENT: QUIMBIOTEC C.A. ART DIRECTOR: EDUARDO CHUMACEIRO DESIGNER: EDUARDO CHUMACEIRO COUNTRY: VENEZUELA INDUSTRY: SCIENTIFIC RESEARCH COMPANY – WISSENSCHAFTLICHE FORSCHUNG – RECHERCHE SCIENTIFIQUE ■ 3 CLIENT: DUDNYK ADVERTISING DESIGN FIRM: NAYLOR, DEDONATO & WOLF ART DIRECTOR/DESIGNER: FRANK PILEGGI COUNTRY: USA INDUSTRY: MARKETING AWARENESS PROGRAM – MARKETING-PROGRAMM – PROGRAMME DE MARKETING ■ 4 CLIENT: THE INSIGHT GROUP DESIGN FIRM: ARROWOOD DESIGN ART DIRECTOR/DESIGNER: SCOTT ARROWOOD COUNTRY: USA INDUSTRY: FINANCIAL PLAN-NERS – FINANZBERATER – CONSEILLERS FINANCIERS ■ 5 CLIENT: Q & A DESIGN FIRM: KARNES PRICKETT DESIGN DESIGNER: DAVE PRICKETT COUNTRY: USA INDUSTRY: MARKETING CONSULTANTS – MARKETING-BERATUNG – CONSEIL EN MARKETING ■ 6 CLIENT: VOLINIK PATENDIBÜROO DESIGN FIRM: VAAL DESIGN ART DIRECTOR/DESIGNER/ILLUSTRATOR: HEINO PRUNSVELT COUNTRY: ESTONIA INDUSTRY: PATENT OFFICE – PATENTBÜRO – INSTITUT DE LA PROPRÉTÉ INDUSTRIELLE ■ 7 CLIENT: NEW ENGLAND ADJUSTERS DESIGN FIRM: FRANK C. LIONETTI DESIGN, INC. ART DIRECTOR: FRANK C. LIONETTI DESIGNER: LAURIE FRICK COUNTRY:

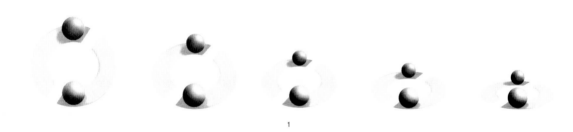

1

USA INDUSTRY: CLAIMS ADJUSTERS FOR DISASTERS – SCHADENSSACHVERSTÄNDIGE BEI KATASTROPHEN – AGENT GÉNÉRAL D'ASSURANCES SPÉCIALISÉ DANS LES SINISTRES ■ 8 CLIENT: I-SERV DESIGN FIRM: GRAPHIC COMMUNICATION CONCEPTS ART DIRECTOR/DESIGNER: SUDARSHAN DHEER COUNTRY: INDIA INDUSTRY: SERVICE COMPANY – DIENSTLEISTUNGSUNTERNEHMEN ■ 9 CLIENT: SUSAN SNOWE DESIGNER: PHILIP QUINN COUNTRY: USA INDUSTRY: PERSONAL DEVELOPMENT CONSULTANT – INDIVIDUELLE BERATUNG – SERVICE DE CONSEIL PERSONNALISÉ ■ 10 CLIENT: SACCESS INCORPORATED DESIGN FIRM: GRANT JORGENSEN GRAPHIC DESIGN ART DIRECTOR/DESIGNER: GRANT JORGENSEN COUNTRY: AUSTRALIA INDUSTRY: CONSULTANCY SERVICES – BERA-TUNGSDIENST – SOCIÉTÉ DE CONSEIL ■ 11 CLIENT: VITRIA TECHNOLOGY, INC. DESIGN FIRM: EARL GEE DESIGN ART DIRECTOR/ILLUSTRATOR: EARL GEE DESIGNERS: EARL GEE, FANI CHUNG COUNTRY: USA INDUSTRY: HIGH TECHNOL-OGY CONSULTING – TECHNOLOGISCHE BERATUNG – CONSEIL EN TECHNOLOGY – SOCIÉTÉ DE CONSEIL EN TECHNOLOGIE ■ 12 CLIENT: MELROSE CONSULTING DESIGN FIRM: RICKABAUGH GRAPHICS ART DIRECTOR: ERIC RICKABAUGH DESIGNER: TINA ZIENTARSKI COUNTRY: USA INDUSTRY: CONSULTING, INVESTOR RELATIONS – ANLAGEBERATUNG – SOCIÉTÉ DE CONSEIL EN PLACEMENTS ■ 13 CLIENT: I.N. SOLUTIONS DESIGN FIRM: PETERSON & COMPANY ART DIRECTOR/DESIGNER: SCOTT RAY COUNTRY: USA INDUSTRY: CONSULTANT FIRM FOR HIGH-TECH COR-PORATIONS – BERATUNG FÜR HIGH-TECH-FIRMEN – SOCIÉTÉ DE CONSEIL POUR ENTREPRISES HIGH-TECH

2

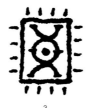

3

4

5

6

7

8

9

10

11

12

13

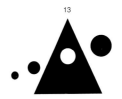

1

2

3

4

5

6

7

8

9

1 Client: PHOTOQUIP INDIA LTD. Design Firm: GRAPHIC COMMUNICATION CONCEPTS Art Director/Designer: SUDARSHAN DHEER Country: INDIA Description: PHOTOGRAPHIC PRODUCTS – PHOTOGRAPHISCHE PRODUKTE – PRODUITS PHOTOGRAPHIQUES ■ **2** Client: STEFAN RACHBAUER Art Director/Designer: BORIS BERGHAMMER Country: AUSTRIA Description: TECHNO FASHION STORE – TECHNO-MODEBOUTIQUE – BOUTIQUE TECHNO ■ **3** Client: TENGFEN HOLDINGS CO. LTD. Design Firm: YE DESIGN Art Director: XIAO YONG Designer: XIAO YONG Country: CHINA Description: MACHINERY INDUSTRY – MASCHINENINDUSTRIE – INDUSTRIE MÉCANIQUE ■ **4** Client: SUNJOY CORPORATION Design Firm: LESLIE CHAN DESIGN CO., LTD. Art Director: LESLIE CHAN WING KEI Designer: LESLIE CHAN WING KEI Country: TAIWAN Description: DIRECT SELLING – DIREKTVERKAUF – VENTE DIRECTE ■ **5** Client: NÉPBOLT RT. Design Firm: ART FORCE STUDIO Art Director/ Designer: ATTILA SIMON Illustrator: DANIEL HORVATH Country: HUNGARY Description: BUSINESS FIRM – GESCHÄFTLICHE UNTERNEHMUNG – SOCIÉTÉ COMMERCIALES ■ **6** Client: HOT WAVE AUSTRIA Art Director/Designer: BORIS BERGHAMMER Country: AUSTRIA Description: FASHION SHOP – BEKLEIDUNGS-

10

GESCHÄFT – BOUTIQUE DE MODE ■ **7** Client: DONGHA CORP. Design Firm: YE DESIGN Art Director/Designer: XIAO YONG Country: CHINA Description: TRADE – HANDEL – COMMERCE ■ **8** Client: INTERMATION CORPORATION Design Firm: HORNALL ANDERSON DESIGN WORKS Art Director: JACK ANDERSON Designers: JACK ANDERSON, JULIA LAPINE, JILL BUSTAMANTE Illustrator: JULIA LAPINE Country: USA Description: INFORMATION STORAGE AND RETRIEVAL/SPEICHERUNG UND ABRUFUNG VON INFORMATIONEN ■ **9** Client: FEDERAL COMPLIANCE CORPORATION Design Firm: DESIGNWORKS Art Director: STEVE ST. JOHN Designer: STEVE ST. JOHN Country: USA Description: BUSINESS CONSULTANTS FOR COMPLYING WITH THE AMERICAN DISABILITIES ACT – FIRMENBERATUNG IN BEZUG AUF DAS AMERIKANISCHE BEHINDERTENGESETZ – SOCIÉTÉ DE CONSEIL SPÉCIALISÉE DANS LA LOI AMÉRICAINE SUR LES INVALIDES ■ **10** Client: THE CZECH TECHNOLOGY PARK, BRNO A.S. Design Firm: ROUNDEL DESIGN GROUP Art Director: MICHAEL DENNY Designers: JOHN BATESON, DEBORAH OSBORNE, ANDREW ROSS, JONATHAN SIMPSON, RACHAEL DINNIS Country: CZECH REPUBLIC Description: TECHNOLOGY PARK – TECHNOLOGIE-PARK – PARC TECHNOLOGIQUE

1 Client: THE DALLAS OPERA GUILD Design Firm: JOSEPH RATTAN DESIGN Art Director: JOSEPH RATTAN Designer: GREG MORGAN, JOSEPH RATTAN Illustrator: GREG MORGAN Country: USA Purpose: INVITATION TO A WINE AUCTION BENEFITING THE DALLAS OPERA GUILD – EINLADUNG ZU EINER WEINAUKTION ZUGUNSTEN DER OPER VON DALLAS – INVITATION À UNE VENTE AUX ENCHÈRES DE VINS AU BÉNÉFICE DE L'OPÉRA DE DALLAS. ■ **2** Client: COLLIER CAMPBELL Design Firm: WPS DESIGN GROUP Art Director: GAIL RIGELHAUPT Designer: STEPHAN WALTER Country: USA Industry: HOME FURNISHING MANUFACTURER – HERSTEL-

1

LER VON EINRICHTUNGSGEGENSTÄNDEN – FABRICANT D'OBJETS DE DÉCORATION D'INTÉRIEUR ■ **3** Client: FERDINAND ANYS Art Director/Designer/Illustrator: BORIS BERGHAMMER Country: AUSTRIA Industry: ASSEMBLY METAL WORKING – MONTAGESCHLOSSEREI – ATELIER D'AJUSTAGE ■ **4** Client: STEPHEN BENNION Design Firm: SMIT GHORMLEY LOFGREEN DESIGN Art Director/Designer: ART LOFGREEN Country: USA Industry: FURNITURE MAKER – MÖBELHERSTELLER – FABRICANT DE MEUBLES ■ **5** Client: RED ROOF FARM ANTIQUES Design Firm: SWIETER DESIGN N.W. Art Director: JOHN SWIETER Designer: JOHN SWIETER, PAUL MUNSTERMAN Illustrator: PAUL MUNSTERMAN Country: USA Industry: ANTIQUES – ANTIQUITÄTEN – ANTIQUITÉS

2

3

4

5

1

2

3

4

1 CLIENT: DIANE HANDS OUT OF HAND DESIGN FIRM: HALEY JOHNSON DESIGN CO. DESIGNER/ILLUSTRATOR: HALEY JOHNSON COUNTRY: USA INDUSTRY/PURPOSE: CRAFTED HANDMADE TILES – HANDGEMACHTE FLIESEN – CARRELAGES DE FABRICATION ARTISANALE ■ **2** CLIENT: MENOYA DESIGN FIRM: SHIN MATSUNAGA DESIGN INC. ART DIRECTOR/DESIGNER: SHIN MATSUNAGA COUNTRY: JAPAN INDUSTRY/PURPOSE: JEWELRY – SCHMUCK – BIJOUTERIE ■ **3** CLIENT: ROSWELL BOOKBINDING DESIGN FIRM: SMIT GHORMLEY LOFGREEN DESIGN ART

5

DIRECTOR/ DESIGNER: BRAD GHORMLEY COUNTRY: USA INDUSTRY/PURPOSE: BOOKBINDER – BUCHBINDER – RELIEUR ■ **4** CLIENT: DIAN NEEDHAM FURNITURE DESIGN FIRM: CHRIS NEEDHAM DESIGN DESIGNER: CHRIS NEEDHAM COUNTRY: USA INDUSTRY/PURPOSE: FURNITURE DESIGNER – MÖBELDESIGNER – DESIGNER DE MEUBLES ■ **5** CLIENT: FA. STROBEL DESIGN FIRM: BÜRO FÜR GESTALTUNG ART DIRECTOR/DESIGNER: MARTIN HUBER PHOTOGRAPHER: STEFAN IBELE COUNTRY: GERMANY INDUSTRY/PURPOSE: CARPENTER – SCHREINEREI – MENUISERIE

CREATIVE SERVICES·KREATIVE DIENSTE·SERVICES CRÉATIFS

1

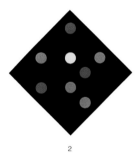

2

3

1 CLIENT: M.G. SWING COMPANY DESIGN FIRM: MIRES DESIGN, INC. ART DIRECTOR: JOSÉ SERRANO DESIGNER: SCOTT MIRES, JOSÉ SERRANO COUNTRY: USA INDUSTRY/PURPOSE: PAINTING CONTRACTOR SPECIALIZING IN FAUX FINISHES – AUF IMITATIONEN SPEZIALISIERTER MALERBETRIEB – ENTREPRISE DE PAINTEUR ORNE-MANISTE ■ 2 CLIENT: JÖRG ALEXANDER ZAUBERKUNST DESIGNER: CARSTEN ABELBECK COUNTRY: GERMANY

full moon event productions, inc.

4

INDUSTRY/PURPOSE: MAGICIAN – ZAUBERKÜNSTLER – MAGICIEN ■ 3 CLIENT: AFTAB CO. DESIGN FIRM: ASHENA ADVERTISING ART DIRECTOR: IRAJ MIRZA-ALIKHANI DESIGNER: LADAN REZAEI COUNTRY: IRAN PURPOSE: LOGO BASED ON IRANIAN ALPHABET(A) – LOGO AUF DER BASIS DES IRANISCHEN ALPHABETS (A) – LOGO BASÉ SUR L'ALPHABET IRANIEN ■ 4 CLIENT: FULL MOON EVENT PRODUCTION DESIGN FIRM: THE LEONHARDT GROUP DESIGNER: TRACI DABERKO COUNTRY: USA INDUSTRY/PURPOSE: EVENT PLANNING, CONFERENCE ORGANIZER

1

2

3

4

5

1 CLIENT: T. RADCLIFFE MIGNEREY DESIGN FIRM: DESIGN GUYS ART DIRECTOR/DESIGNER/ILLUSTRATOR: RICHARD BOYNTON COUNTRY: USA INDUSTRY/PURPOSE: COPYWRITER – TEXTER – RÉDACTEUR PUBLICITAIRE ■ 2 CLIENT: BENJAMIN MIDDAUGH DESIGN FIRM: DOGSTAR DESIGN DESIGNER/ILLUSTRATOR: RODNEY DAVIDSON COUNTRY: USA BUSINESS: VOICE TEACHER – SPRACHLEHRER – PROFESSEUR DE LANGUE ■ 3 CLIENT: LUNAISON GBR DESIGN FIRM: FACTOR DESIGN ART DIRECTOR/DESIGNER/ILLUSTRATOR: RÜDIGER GÖTZ COUNTRY: GERMANY INDUSTRY: DISTRIBUTION OF LAMPS – LAMPENVERTRIEB – SOCIÉTÉ DE DISTRIBUTION DE LUNINAIRES ■ 4

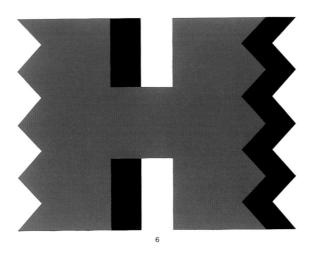

6

CLIENT: HOHMANN PAINTING & DECORATING DESIGNER: ASTRID BECHER COUNTRY: USA INDUSTRY/PURPOSE: PAINTING AND DECORATING – MALER- UND EINRICHTUNGSGESCHÄFT – ENTREPRISE DE PEINTURE ET DE DÉCORATION ■ 5 CLIENT/DESIGN FIRM: VOX ADVERTISING & DESIGN ART DIRECTOR: DREW ALLISON, DAVID WEINSTEIN COUNTRY: USA BUSINESS: BOUTIQUE CREATIVE SERVICES – WERBUNG UND DESIGN – AGENCE DE PUBLICITÉ ET DE DESIGN ■ 6 CLIENT: HINRICHS BEKLEIDUNGSWERKE GMBH DESIGN FIRM: DESIGN KONNEX ART DIRECTOR/DESIGNER: SYLVIA FREIDLER COUNTRY: GERMANY BUSINESS: APPAREL – BEKLEIDUNG – VÊTEMENTS

1 Client: ANGELIC BREWING COMPANY Design Firm: PLANET DESIGN COMPANY Art Directors: DANA LYTLE, KEVIN WADE Designer: DANA LYTLE Country: USA Industry/Purpose: BREWERY, RESTAURANT – BRAUEREI, RESTAURANT – BRASSERIE ■ 2 Client: BITTER END BISTRO & BREWERY Design Firm: HIXO, INC. Art Director/Designer: MIKE HICKS Country: USA Industry/Purpose: RESTAURANT, BREWERY – RESTAURANT, BRAUEREI – BRASSERIE ■ 3 Client: LIVERPOOL RESTAURANT & PUB Design Firm: FREE RANGE DESIGN Designer: DAVID HUGHES Country: USA Industry/Purpose: RESTAURANT ■ 4 Client: RUBIO'S RESTAURANTS, INC. Design Firm: MIRES DESIGN, INC. Art Director/Designer: JOHN BALL Country: USA Industry/Purpose: FAST FOOD – SCHNELLIMBISS ■ 5 Client: MILL CREEK BREWERY Design Firm: BARKLEY & EVERGREEN Creative Director: CRAIG NEUMAN Designers: EDD TIMMONS, PAUL DIAMOND Illustrator: NANCY STAHL Country: USA Industry/Purpose: BREWERY, RESTAURANT – BRAUEREI, RESTAURANT – BRASSERIE ■ 6 Client: TEIGWAREN RIESA GMBH Design Firm: DESIGN KONNEX Art Directors/Designers: SYLVIA FREIDLER, KONSTANTIN KERN Illustrator: MARCUS GSCHWENDTNER Country: GERMANY Industry/Purpose: NOODLE MANUFACTURER – TEIGWARENHERSTELLER – FABRICANT DE PÂTES ALIMENTAIRES ■ 7 Client: SOUTH COAST VINTNERS ASSOCIATION Design Firm: MIRES DESIGN Art Director/Designer: JOHN BALL Country: USA Industry/Purpose: CONSORTIUM OF REGIONAL WINERIES – WINZERVERBAND – ASSOCIATION DE VIGNERONS ■ 8 Client: THE FOOD GROUP Design Firm: MIRES DESIGN, INC. Art Director: SCOTT MIRES Designers: SCOTT MIRES, MIKE BROWER Illustrator: TRACY SABIN Country: USA Industry/Purpose: FOOD PRODUCT

1

PROMOTION – PROMOTION VON LEBENSMITTELN – PROMOTION DE PRODUITS ALIMENTAIRES ■ 9 Client: OAK VALLEY/DC&A Design Firm/Art Director/Designer: POINT ZERO Country: KOREA Industry/Purpose: RESORT AREA AND GOLF COURSE – ERHOLUNGSGEBIET UND GOLFANLAGE – LIEU DE VILLÉGIATURE ET TERRAIN DE GOLF ■ 10 Client: TACO PRONTO Design Firm: MIRES DESIGN, INC. Art Director/Designer: SCOTT MIRES Country: USA Industry/Purpose: FAST FOOD RESTAURANT – SCHNELLIMBISS ■ 11 Client: NEW YORK TIMES, PHIL PATLON Design Firm: CHARLES S. ANDERSON DESIGN COMPANY Art Director: CHARLES S. ANDERSON Designers: CHARLES S. ANDERSON, ERIK JOHNSON Illustrator: ERIK JOHNSON Country: USA Industry/Purpose: FOOD PRODUCTS – NAHRUNGSMITTEL – PRODUITS ALIMENTAIRES ■ 12 Client: CHICAGO DOG AND DELI Design Firm: SAYLES GRAPHIC DESIGN Art Director/Designer/Illustrator: JOHN SAYLES Country: USA Industry/Purpose: UPSCALE DELI – DELIKATESSENGESCHÄFT – TRAITEUR ■ 13 Client: AQUA CUISINE Design Firm/Designer/Illustrator: MICHAEL SCHWAB DESIGN Art Director: DOUG GILMOUR Country: USA Industry/Purpose: RESTAURANT ■ 14 Client: HIDES BAR & GRILL Design Firm: HARCUS DESIGN Art Director: ANNETTE HARCUS Designer/Illustrator: MARIO MILOSTIC Country: AUSTRALIA Industry/Purpose: BAR AND GRILL RESTAURANT – BAR UND RESTAURANT – BAR ET RÔTISSERIE ■ 15 Client: HEALTHY CHEF Design Firm: THE HILL GROUP Art Director: CHRIS HILL Designer: EDDIE TAMEZ Country: USA Industry/Purpose: CATERER – GASTRONOM – TRAITEUR ■ 16 Client: STEINBRUCH CAFÉ RESTAURANT Design Firm: DESIGN AHEAD Designer: RALF STUMPF Country: GERMANY Industry/Purpose: RESTAURANT

2

3

4

5

6

7

8

9

10

11

12

13

14

15

16

CULINARY · KULINARISCH · CUISINE

1 CLIENT: MADRIGAL DINNERS ART DIRECTOR/DESIGNER/ILLUSTRATOR: BRIAN LARSON COUNTRY: USA INDUSTRY/PURPOSE: CATERER – GASTRONOMIE – TRAITEUR ■ **2** CLIENT: WINTERBROOK INC. DESIGN FIRM: NANCY STENTZ DESIGN ART DIRECTOR/DESIGNER/ILLUSTRATOR: NANCY STENTZ COUNTRY: USA INDUSTRY/PURPOSE: SOFT DRINK MANUFACTURER – HERSTELLER VON ERFRISCHUNGSGETRÄNKEN – FABRICANT DE SODAS ■ **3** CLIENT: AMAZON CLUB AND PIRANHA BAR DESIGN FIRM: GIBBS BARONET ART DIRECTOR/DESIGNER: STEVE GIBBS COUNTRY: USA INDUSTRY/PURPOSE: CLUB AND BAR ■ **4** CLIENT: CANDINAS CHOCOLATIER DESIGN FIRM: PLANET DESIGN COMPANY ART DIRECTORS: KEVIN WADE, DANA LYTLE DESIGNER: KEVIN WADE COUNTRY: USA

1

INDUSTRY/PURPOSE: CHOCOLATE COMPANY, RETAILER – VERKAUF VON SCHOKOLADE – CHOCOLATIER ■ **5** CLIENT: KEBA GMBH DESIGN FIRM: KEITH HARRIS PACKAGE DESIGN ART DIRECTOR/DESIGNER: KEITH HARRIS ILLUSTRATOR: KEITH HARRIS COUNTRY: GERMANY INDUSTRY/PURPOSE: FOOD MANUFACTURER – LEBENSMITTEL-HERSTELLER – FABRICANT DE PRODUITS ALIMENTAIRES ■ **6** CLIENT: AJAX TAVERN DESIGN FIRM: MICHAEL SCHWAB DESIGN ART DIRECTOR: BILL HIGGINS DESIGNER/ILLUSTRATOR: MICHAEL SCHWAB COUNTRY: USA BUSINESS RESTAURANT AT THE FOOT OF AJAX MOUNTAIN IN ASPEN – RESTAURANT AM FUSSE DES BERGES AJAX IN ASPEN, COLORADO – RESTAURANT SITUÉ AU PIED DU MONT AJAX À ASPEN DANS LE COLORADO

2

3

4

5

6

1

2

3

4

5

6

7

8

9

10

11

12

13

14

15

1 CLIENT: HEALTHY CHEF DESIGN FIRM: THE HILL GROUP ART DIRECTOR: CHRIS HILL DESIGNER: TOM BERNO COUNTRY: USA PURPOSE: CATERER – GASTRONOM – TRAITEUR ■ **2** CLIENT: BUFFALO CONNECTION DESIGN FIRM: DOGSTAR DESIGN DESIGNER/ILLUSTRATOR: RODNEY DAVIDSON COUNTRY: USA INDUSTRY: RESTAURANT ■ **3** CLIENT: PORTLAND BREWING DESIGN FIRM: SANDSTROM DESIGN ART DIRECTOR/DESIGNER: SALLY HARTMAN MORROW ILLUSTRATOR: JANÉE WARREN COUNTRY: USA INDUSTRY: MICROBREWERY – KLEIN-BRAUEREI – MINI-BRASSERIE ■ **4** CLIENT: BENNIGAN'S DESIGN FIRM: DENNARD CREATIVE ART DIRECTOR/DESIGNER: BOB DENNARD ILLUSTRATOR: JAMES LACEY COUNTRY: USA INDUSTRY: RESTAURANT ■ **5** CLIENT: F.B.I. CO. LTD. DESIGN FIRM: ROUND TABLE ASSOCIATES INC. ART DIRECTOR: MASUMI OHASHI DESIGNER: NAONOBU NAKAMURA COUNTRY: USA INDUSTRY: RESTAURANT ■ **6** CLIENT: BENNIGAN'S IRISH AMERICAN TAVERN DESIGN FIRM: DENNARD CREATIVE ART DIRECTOR/DESIGNER: BOB DENNARD ILLUSTRATOR: JAMES LACEY COUNTRY: USA INDUSTRY: RESTAURANT ■ **7–9** CLIENT: SWEETISH HILL BAKERY DESIGN FIRM: HIXO, INC. ART DIRECTOR: TOM POTH DESIGNERS: TOM POTH, MIKE HICKS COUNTRY: USA INDUSTRY: BAKERY – BÄCKEREI – BOULANGERIE ■ **10** CLIENT: DEATH VALLEY CHILI COMPANY DESIGN FIRM: PENNEBAKER DESIGN ART DIRECTOR: DAVID LERCH, WARD PENNEBAKER DESIGNER: DAVID LERCH COUNTRY: USA

THE STONE KITCHEN

16

INDUSTRY: FOOD – NAHRUNGSMITTEL – PRODUITS ALIMENTAIRES ■ **11** CLIENT: LIPPERT WILKENS PARTNER DESIGN FIRM: KEITH HARRIS PACKAGE DESIGN ART DIRECTOR/DESIGNER/ILLUSTRATOR: KEITH HARRIS COUNTRY: GERMANY INDUSTRY: FAST FOOD – SCHNELLGERICHTE ■ **12** CLIENT: NEW YORK TIMES, PHIL PATLON DESIGN FIRM: CHARLES S ANDERSON DESIGN CO. ART DIRECTOR: CHARLES S. ANDERSON DESIGNERS: CHARLES S. ANDERSON, ERIK JOHNSON ILLUSTRATOR: ERIK JOHNSON COUNTRY: USA INDUSTRY: FOOD PRODUCTS – NAHRUNGSMITTEL – PRODUITS ALIMENTAIRES ■ **13** CLIENT: GINGER CLUB INC. DESIGN FIRM: CORNELL DESIGN ART DIRECTOR/DESIGNER: ALBERT TRESKIN COUNTRY: USA INDUSTRY: RESTAURANT ■ **14** CLIENTS: JOELL PLATT, LEO WARFIELD DESIGN FIRM: MICHAEL STANARD INC. ART DIRECTOR: MICHAEL STANARD DESIGNER: MARC. C. FUHRMAN COUNTRY: USA INDUSTRY: RESTAURANT, BAR AND SPORTS MUSEUM – RESTAURANT, BAR UND SPORTMUSEUM – RESTAURANT, BAR ET MUSÉE DU SPORT ■ **15** CLIENT: MADISON SOURDOUGH DESIGN FIRM: PLANET DESIGN COMPANY ART DIRECTOR: KEVIN WADE, DANA LYTLE DESIGNER: DANA LYTLE COUNTRY: USA INDUSTRY: BAKERY – BÄCKEREI – BOULANGERIE ■ **16** CLIENT: THE STONE KITCHEN DESIGN FIRM: GEER DESIGN, INC. ART DIRECTOR/DESIGNER/ILLUSTRATOR: MARK GEER COUNTRY: USA INDUSTRY: CATERING COMPANY – GASTRONOMISCHER BETRIEB – SERVICE-TRAITEUR

1 CLIENT: CASCADE RESTAURANT DESIGN FIRM: ART FORCE STUDIO ART DIRECTOR/DESIGNER: JUDIT TOTH COUNTRY: HUNGARY INDUSTRY/PURPOSE: RESTAURANT ■ 2 CLIENT: CAFE EXPRESS DESIGN FIRM: HILL/A MARKETING DESIGN GROUP, INC. ART DIRECTOR: CHRIS HILL DESIGNER: JEFF DAVIS COUNTRY: USA INDUSTRY/ PURPOSE: CAFE – KAFFEEHAUS – MAISON DU CAFÉ ■ 3 CLIENT: ZIO RICCO DESIGN FIRM: THE LEONHARDT GROUP DESIGNERS: JANET KRUSE, TRACI DABERKO COUNTRY: USA INDUSTRY/PURPOSE: COFFEE HOUSE – KAFFEEHAUS – MAISON DU CAFÉ ■ 4 CLIENT: THE COCA-COLA COMPANY DESIGN FIRM: DUFFY DESIGN ART DIRECTOR: JOE DUFFY DESIGNERS: KOBE, NEIL POWELL, ALAN LEUSINK COUNTRY: USA INDUSTRY/PURPOSE: SOFT DRINKS – ERFRISCHUNGSGETRÄNKE – SODAS ■ 5 CLIENT: 801 STEAK & CHOP HOUSE DESIGN FIRM: SAYLES GRAPHIC DESIGN ART DIRECTOR/DESIGNER/ILLUSTRATOR: JOHN SAYLES COUNTRY: USA BUSINESS: RESTAURANT ■ 6 CLIENT: MISSION RIDGE DESIGN FIRM: HORNALL ANDERSON DESIGN WORKS, INC. ART DIRECTOR: JACK ANDERSON DESIGNERS: JACK ANDERSON, CLIFF CHUNG, DENISE WEIR, DAVID BATES, LEO RAYMUNDO LETTERER: GEORGE TANAGI COUNTRY: USA INDUSTRY/PURPOSE: SKI RESORT – WINTERSPORTORT – STATION DE SPORTS D'HIVER ■ 7 CLIENT: JAVA JOES DESIGN FIRM: SAYLES GRAPHIC DESIGN ART DIRECTOR: JOHN SAYLES DESIGNER/ILLUSTRATOR: JOHN SAYLES COUNTRY: USA INDUSTRY/PURPOSE: COFFEE HOUSE – KAFFEEHAUS – MAISON DU CAFÉ ■ 8 CLIENT: THE PALACE OF THE LOST CITY DESIGN FIRM: DAVID CARTER DESIGN ART DIRECTOR: RANDALL HILL DESIGNER/ILLUSTRATOR: BRIAN MOSS COUNTRY: BOPHUTHATSWANA BUSINESS: BAR ■ 9 CLIENT: HOTEL VIRU DESIGN FIRM: VAAL DESIGN ART DIRECTOR/DESIGNER: HEINO PRUNSVELT ILLUSTRATOR:

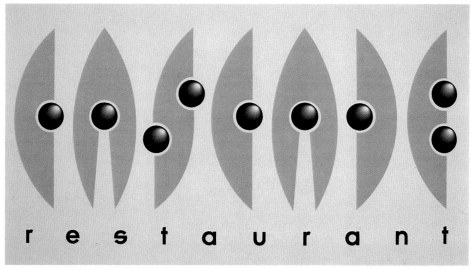

1

HEINO PRUNSVELT COUNTRY: ESTONIA INDUSTRY/PURPOSE: RESTAURANT ■ 10 CLIENT: DANTE'S RESTAURANTS, INC. DESIGN FIRM: SOMMESE DESIGN ART DIRECTOR/DESIGNER/ILLUSTRATOR: LANNY SOMMESE COMPUTER DESIGN: STEVE EALEY COUNTRY: USA INDUSTRY/PURPOSE: RESTAURANT WITH TWO CHEFS NAMED MARIO AND LUIGI – RESTAURANT MIT ZWEI KÜCHENCHEFS NAMENS MARIO UND LUIGI – MARIO ET LUIGI, LES DEUX MAÎTRES-QUEUX DU RESTAURANT ■ 11 CLIENT: HOTEL SUSI DESIGN FIRM: VAAL DESIGN ART DIRECTOR/DESIGNER/ILLUSTRATOR: HEINO PRUNSVELT COUNTRY: ESTONIA INDUSTRY/PURPOSE: NIGHT CLUB – NACHTCLUB – NIGHT-CLUB ■ 12 CLIENT: ALAN JACKSON DESIGN FIRM: VRONTIKIS DESIGN OFFICE ART DIRECTOR: PETRULA VRONTIKIS DESIGNER: KIM SAGE COUNTRY: USA INDUSTRY/PURPOSE: RESTAURANT ■ 13 CLIENT: URBAN DESIGN & ARCHITECTURE, CITY OF MELBOURNE DESIGN FIRM: INHOUSE DESIGN CITY OF MELBOURNE ART DIRECTOR/DESIGNER: DEREK SAMUEL ILLUSTRATOR: DEREK SAMUEL COUNTRY: AUSTRALIA INDUSTRY/PURPOSE: LOCAL GOVERNMENT INITIATIVE, KIOSK IN PUBLIC RECREATION SPACE – KIOSK IM ÖFFENTLICHEN ERHOLUNGSRAUM, REGIONALE REGIERUNGSINITIATIVE – KIOSQUE DANS UN LIEU PUBLIQUE, PROJET MUNICIPAL ■ 14 CLIENT: HOTEL PACIFICA DESIGN FIRM: HAKUHODO, INC. ART DIRECTOR/DESIGNER: JAY VIGON ILLUSTRATOR: JAY VIGON COUNTRY: JAPAN INDUSTRY/PURPOSE: RESTAURANT ■ 15 CLIENT: THE COCA-COLA COMPANY DESIGN FIRM: DUFFY DESIGN ART DIRECTOR/DESIGNER: JEFF JOHNSON ILLUSTRATOR: JEFF JOHNSON COUNTRY: USA INDUSTRY/PURPOSE: SOFT DRINK – ERFRISCHUNGSGETRÄNKE – SODAS ■ 16 CLIENT: RAINFOREST CAFE DESIGN FIRM: THE LEONHARDT GROUP ART DIRECTOR: DENNIS CLOUSE DESIGNERS: TRACI DABERKO, DENNIS CLOUSE COUNTRY: USA BUSINESS: RESTAURANT IN ZOO – RESTAURANT IM ZOO – RESTAURANT DU ZOO

2

3

4

5

6

7

TUSK BAR

8

9

10

11

12

CAFE L'INCONTRO

13

14

15

16

1

2

3

4

5

6

7

8

9

10

11

12

13

1 Client: JEFF'S MARINA CAFE Design Firm: HIXO, INC. Art Director: MIKE HICKS Designer: BILL GEISLER Country: USA Industry/Purpose: RESTAURANT ■ **2** Client: JOHNSON OIL CO. Design Firm: YOUNG + LARAMORE Creative Directors: DAVID YOUNG, JEFF LARAMORE Art Director: CHRIS BEATTY Writer: SCOTT MONTGOMERY Country: USA Industry/Purpose: COFFEE AT CONVENIENCE STORES – LÄDEN MIT KAFFEE UND FERTIGGERICHTEN – MAGASINS AVEC BARS À CAFÉ ■ **3** Client: SEATTLE CHOCOLATES Design Firm: BARNES & ASSOCIATES Art Director: KEITH BARNES Designer/Illustrator: NANCY STENTZ Country: USA Industry: CHOCOLATE MANUFACTURER – HERSTELLER VON SCHOKOLADE – CHOCOLATIER ■ **4** Client: DAKA INTER- NATIONAL Design Firm: SULLIVANPERKINS Art Director/Designer/Illustrator: ART GARCIA Country: USA Business: CATERING COMPANY – GASTRONOMISCHER BETRIEB – SERVICE-TRAITEUR ■ **5** Client: CHICKEN- VILLE RESTAURANT Design Firm: SANDSTROM DESIGN Art Director/Designer: STEVEN SANDSTROM Country: USA Business: FAST FOOD RESTAURANT – SCHNELLIMBISS – FAST-FOOD ■ **5** Client: BEER BOY ENTERPRISES Design Firm: MACVICAR DESIGN AND COMMUNICATIONS Art Director: JOHN VANCE Designer/Illustrator: JOHN VANCE Country: USA Industry/Purpose: HOME BEER BREWING KITS AND SUPPLIES – GERÄTE ZUR PRI- VATEN BIERBRAUEREI – PETIT KIT ET USTENSILES DU PARFAIT BRASSEUR ■ **6** Client: KEBA GMBH Design Firm: KEITH HARRIS PACKAGE DESIGN Art Director/Designer/Illustrator: KEITH HARRIS Country: GERMANY Industry/Purpose: FAST FOOD – SCHNELLIMBISS ■ **7** Client: JO BAR AND ROTISSERIE Design Firm: PRINCIPIA

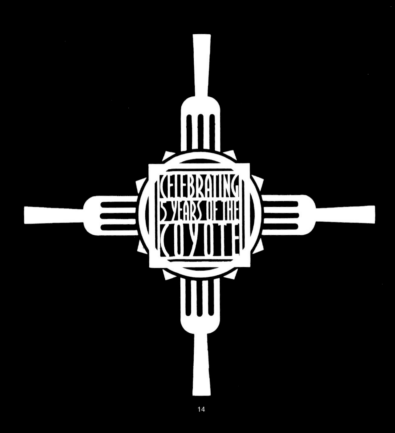

14

GRAPHICA Art Directors: ROBIN RICKABAUGH, HEIDI RICKABAUGH Designers: JON OLSEN, ROBIN RICKABAUGH Country: USA Industry/Purpose: RESTAURANT ■ **8** Client: CHAUCER'S Design Firm: BREMMER & GORIS COMMUNICATIONS, INC. Art Director: DENNIS GORIS Designer/Illustrator: LAURA BEIRNE Country: USA Industry/Purpose: RESTAURANT WITH MEDIEVAL THEME – RESTAURANT MIT MITTELALTERLICHEM THEMA – RESTAURANT «MÉDIÉVAL» ■ **9** Client: TRAFFIC CAFE Design Firm: PHOENIX CREATIVE Art Director: ERIC THOELKE Designer/Illustrator: KATHY WILKINSON Country: USA Industry/Purpose: COFFEE SHOP – CAFÉ ■ **10** Client: METZ BAKING COMPANY Design Firm: DOTZLER DESIGN Art Director: RAY DOTZLER Designer: TODD EBY Country: USA Industry/Purpose: BAKERY – BÄCKEREI – BOULANGERIE ■ **11** Clients: JAVA THE HUT, JON STECKLER Design Firm: HEWARDESIGN Art Director/Designer: HEWARD JUE Country: USA Business: ESPRESSO BAR, FOOD SERVICE – ESPRESSO BAR, HAUSLIEFERDIENST VON LEBENSMITTELN – BAR À CAFÉ, SERVICE-TRAITEUR ■ **12** Client: TOPANGA PLAZA Design Firm: SULLIVANPERKINS Art Director/Designer: ART GARCIA Country: USA Industry/Purpose: RETAIL FOOD COURT – LEBENSMITTELGESCHÄFT – MAGASIN D'ALI- MENTATION ■ **13** Client: COCA-COLA, COFFEE FROST Design Firm: CURTIS DESIGN Art Director: DAVID CURTIS Designer: DAVID CURTIS Illustrator: DAVID CURTIS Country: USA Industry/Purpose: CARBONATED ICED COFFEE DRINK – EISKAFFEEGETRÄNK MIT KOHLENSÄURE – CAFÉ GLACÉ (BOISSON GAZEUSE) ■ **14** Client: PB & J RESTAURANT – COYOTE GRILL Design Firm: EAT DESIGN, L.L.C. Art Director: PATRICK EILTS- JOBE Designer: PATRICK EILTS-JOBE Typographer: KEVIN TRACY Country: USA Business: RESTAURANT

1

2

3

4

5

6

7

8

9

1 CLIENT: LYON LAMB DESIGN FIRM: DESIGN/ART, INC. ART DIRECTOR/DESIGNER: NORMAN MOORE COUNTRY: USA INDUSTRY: VIDEO ANIMATION SYSTEMS – VIDEO-ANIMATIONSSYSTEME – SYSTÈMES D'ANIMENTATIONS VIDÉO ■ **2** CLIENT: ART COMPANY LONDON DESIGN FIRM: PHOENIX CREATIVE ART DIRECTOR: ERIC THOELKE DESIGNER/ILLUSTRATOR: ED MANTELS-SEEKER COUNTRY: USA INDUSTRY/PURPOSE: ART DEALER – KUNSTHANDEL – MARCHANT D'ART ■ **3** CLIENT: OASIS RADIO DESIGN FIRM: RBMM/THE RICHARDS GROUP DESIGNER: WEBB BLEVINS COUNTRY: USA BUSINESS: RADIO STATION – RADIOSENDER – STATION DE RADIO ■ **4** CLIENT: EVANS & SUTHERLAND DESIGN FIRM: CLARKSON CREATIVE ART DIRECTOR/DESIGNER/ILLUSTRATOR: LARRY CLARKSON COUNTRY: USA INDUSTRY: VIRTUAL REALITY AMUSEMENT GAMES – COMPUTERSPIEL – JEUX VIDÉO ■ **5** CLIENT: CANKARJEV DOM DESIGN FIRM: KROG ART DIRECTOR/DESIGNER: EDI BERK COUNTRY: SLOVENIA INDUSTRY/PURPOSE: CULTURAL AND CONGRESS CENTER – KULTUR- UND KONGRESSZENTRUM – CENTRE CULTUREL ■ **6** CLIENT: RADIO ZLIN (GOLDEN DRUM) DESIGN FIRM: RM DESIGN ART DIRECTOR/DESIGNER: RADIM MOJZIS COUNTRY: CZECH

10

REPUBLIC INDUSTRY/PURPOSE: RADIO STATION — RADIOSENDER — STATION DE RADIO ■ 7 CLIENT: ECOPLEX
DESIGN FIRM: DOGSTAR DESIGN ART DIRECTOR: CHARLES BLACK, STEFANIE BECKER DESIGNER/ILLUSTRATOR:
RODNEY DAVIDSON COUNTRY: USA INDUSTRY/PURPOSE: WILD ANIMAL PARK — TIERPARK — PARC ANIMALIER ■ 8
CLIENT: WESTBEACH DESIGN FIRM: DESIGN/ART, INC. ART DIRECTOR/DESIGNER: NORMAN MOORE COUNTRY: USA
INDUSTRY/PURPOSE: RECORDING STUDIO — AUFNAHMESTUDIO — STUDIO D'ENREGISTREMENT ■ 9 CLIENT:
KUNST-FÖRDERUNG DESIGN FIRM: MOTTER-DESIGN DESIGNER: OTHMAR MOTTER COUNTRY: AUSTRIA BUSINESS:
ART PROMOTION — KUNSTFÖRDERUNG — PROMOTION ARTISTIQUE ■ 10–39 CLIENT: TURNER ENTERTAINMENT
DESIGN FIRM: CHARLES S. ANDERSON DESIGN COMPANY ART DIRECTOR: CHARLES S. ANDERSON DESIGNERS:
CHARLES S. ANDERSON, PAUL HOWALT ILLUSTRATORS: CHARLES S. ANDERSON, PAUL HOWALT, JEANIE JENKINS,
ERIK JOHNSON COUNTRY: USA INDUSTRY/PURPOSE: ENTERTAINMENT — UNTERHALTUNG — DIVERTISSEMENTS

1

1 Client: TYPE DIRECTORS CLUB Design Firm: GERARD HUERTA DESIGN, INC. Designer/Illustrator: GERARD HUERTA Country: USA Business: ORGANIZATION OF DESIGNERS AND TYPE DIRECTORS ■ **2** Client/Design Firm: BRAINSTORM Art Directors/Designers: CHUCK JOHNSON, KEN KOESTER Photographer: KEITH BARDIN Illustrator: CHUCK JOHNSON Country: USA Business: DESIGN FIRM – DESIGN-STUDIO – AGENCE DE DESIGN

2

1

2

1 CLIENT/DESIGN FIRM: JOHN SAYLES DESIGN ART DIRECTOR – DESIGNER – ILLUSTRATOR: JOHN SAYLES COUNTRY: USA BUSINESS: DESIGN FIRM – DESIGN-STUDIO – AGENCE DE DESIGN ■ **2** CLIENT/DESIGN FIRM: DESIGN AHEAD DESIGNER: RALF STUMPF COUNTRY: GERMANY INDUSTRY/PURPOSE: DESIGN FIRM – DESIGN-STUDIO – AGENCE DE DESIGN ■ **3** CLIENT/DESIGN FIRM: FIREHOUSE 101 ART + DESIGN DESIGNER/ILLUSTRATOR: KIRK RICHARD SMITH COUNTRY: USA BUSINESS: DESIGN FIRM – DESIGN-STUDIO – AGENCE DE DESIGN ■ **4** CLIENT/ART DIRECTOR/ DESIGNER: MATTHIAS MENCKE COUNTRY: GERMANY BUSINESS: DESIGNER ■ **5** CLIENT/DESIGN FIRM: MICHAEL SCHWAB DESIGN DESIGNER/ILLUSTRATOR: MICHAEL SCHWAB COUNTRY: USA BUSINESS: DESIGN FIRM – DESIGN-STUDIO – AGENCE DE DESIGN ■ **6** CLIENT: SIERRA DESIGNS DESIGN FIRM: CHARLES S. ANDERSON DESIGN COMPANY ART DIRECTOR: CHARLES S. ANDERSON DESIGNERS: CHARLES S. ANDERSON, PAUL HOWALT, TODD PIPER-HAUSWIRTH COUNTRY: USA BUSINESS: CAMPING AND HIKING EQUIPMENT, OUTERWEAR – EQUIPEMENTS D'EXTÉRIEUR

3

4

5

6

1

2

3

4

5

6

7

8

9

10

11

12

13

1—12 Client: CSA ARCHIVE Design Firm: CHARLES S. ANDERSON DESIGN COMPANY Art Director: CHARLES S. ANDERSON Designer: CHARLES S. ANDERSON, ERIK JOHNSON, PAUL HOWALT Country: USA Purpose: ARCHIVE CATALOG — ARCHIVKATALOG — CATALOG D'ARCHIVES ■ 13 Client/Design Firm: DESIGN AHEAD Art Director/Designer: RALF STUMPF Country: GERMANY Business: DESIGN FIRM — DESIGN-STUDIO — AGENCE DE DESIGN

16

1–15 CLIENT/DESIGN FIRM/ILLUSTRATOR: FINISHED ART INC. ART DIRECTOR: DONNA JOHNSTON DESIGNER: KANNEX FUNG COUNTRY: USA BUSINESS: DESIGN FIRM – DESIGN-STUDIO – AGENCE DE DESIGN ■ 16 CLIENT/ ART DIRECTOR/DESIGNER: AZITA PANAHPOUR ILLUSTRATOR: TOM CONNORS COUNTRY: USA BUSINESS: DESIGNER

1 CLIENT/DESIGN FIRM: BRIGHT & ASSOCIATES DESIGNER: KONRAD BRIGHT COUNTRY: USA BUSINESS: DESIGN FIRM — DESIGN-STUDIO — AGENCE DE DESIGN ■ **2** CLIENT/DESIGN FIRM: ART FORCE STUDIO ART DIRECTOR/DESIGNER/ILLUSTRATOR: TAMÁS VERESS COUNTRY: HUNGARY BUSINESS: DESIGN FIRM — DESIGN-STUDIO — AGENCE DE DESIGN ■ **3** CLIENT/DESIGN FIRM: MODERN DOG ART DIRECTOR/DESIGNER/ILLUSTRATOR: VITTORIO COSTARELLA COUNTRY: USA BUSINESS: DESIGN FIRM — DESIGN-STUDIO — AGENCE DE DESIGN ■ **4** CLIENT/DESIGN FIRM: MARK DESIGNS ART DIRECTOR/DESIGNER/PHOTOGRAPHER: MARK LEROY COUNTRY: USA BUSINESS: DESIGN FIRM — DESIGN-STUDIO — AGENCE DE DESIGN ■ **5** CLIENT: THE MERRILL C. BERMAN COLLECTION DESIGN FIRM: MATSUMOTO INCORPORATED ART DIRECTOR/DESIGNER: TAKAAKI MATSUMOTO COUNTRY: USA PURPOSE: COLLECTION OF 20TH CENTURY MODERN ART AND GRAPHIC DESIGN — SAMMLUNG MODERNER KUNST UND GRAPHIK-DESIGNS DES 20. JAHRHUNDERTS — COLLECTION D'ART MODERN DE 20E SIÈCLE ET DESIGN GRAPHIQUE ■ **6** CLIENT: 3 BAGS FULL DESIGN FIRM: ANDREW HOYNE DESIGN ART DIRECTOR/DESIGNER: ANDREW HOYNE ILLUSTRATOR: MICHAEL RAOSS COUNTRY: AUSTRALIA INDUSTRY/PURPOSE: LAUNDRY AND OTHER CASUAL BAGS — WÄSCHE- UND ANDERE SÄCKE ■ **7** CLIENT: DESIGN EDGE, INC. DESIGN FIRM: KILMER, KILMER & JAMES, INC. DESIGNERS: BRENDA KILMER, RICHARD KILMER COUNTRY: USA BUSINESS:

1

DESIGN FIRM — DESIGN-STUDIO — AGENCE DE DESIGN ■ **8** CLIENT: FELIX HELLENKAMP DESIGN FIRM: *)MEDI-AWERK ART DIRECTOR: LUCAS BUCHHOLZ DESIGNER: ZACHARIAS COUNTRY: GERMANY BUSINESS: DESIGNER ■ **9** CLIENT/DESIGN FIRM/ART DIRECTOR/DESIGNER/ILLUSTRATOR: KEN THOMPSON COUNTRY: USA BUSINESS: DESIGNER ■ **10** CLIENT/DESIGN FIRM: SURIC DESIGN STUDIO ART DIRECTOR/DESIGNER/ILLUSTRATOR: YURI SURKOV COUNTRY: RUSSIA BUSINESS: DESIGN FIRM — DESIGN-STUDIO — AGENCE DE DESIGN ■ **11** CLIENT/DESIGN FIRM: BRAINSTORM, INC. ART DIRECTORS/DESIGNERS/ILLUSTRATORS: CHUCK JOHNSON, KEN KOESTER COUNTRY: USA BUSINESS: DESIGN FIRM — DESIGN-STUDIO — AGENCE DE DESIGN ■ **12** CLIENT: ANDREY LOGVIN DESIGN FIRM: LOGVIN DESIGN ART DIRECTOR/DESIGNER/ILLUSTRATOR: ANDREY LOGVIN COUNTRY: RUSSIA BUSINESS: DESIGNER ■ **13** CLIENT/DESIGN FIRM: THINKING CAPS ART DIRECTORS/DESIGNERS: JULIE HENSON, ANN MORTON ILLUSTRATORS: JULIE HENSON, ANN MORTON COUNTRY: USA BUSINESS: DESIGN FIRM — DESIGN-STUDIO — AGENCE DE DESIGN ■ **14** CLIENT/DESIGN FIRM: SUZANNE HELMERICH DESIGN ART DIRECTOR/DESIGNER: SUZANNE HELMERICH COUNTRY: USA BUSINESS: DESIGNER ■ **15** CLIENT/DESIGN FIRM: BRD DESIGN ART DIRECTOR: PETER KING ROBBINS DESIGNER: PETER KING ROBBINS COUNTRY: USA BUSINESS: DESIGN FIRM — DESIGN-STUDIO — AGENCE DE DESIGN ■ **16** CLIENT: ART DIRECTION AND DESIGN DESIGN FIRM: LATITUDE/THE RICHARDS GROUP ART DIRECTOR: FELIX P. SOCKWELL COUNTRY: USA BUSINESS: DESIGN FIRM — DESIGN-STUDIO — AGENCE DE DESIGN

2

3

4

5

6

7

8

9

10

11

12

13

14

15

16

1 C LIENT: BUENA VISTA COLLEGE D ESIGN F IRM: SAYLES GRAPHIC DESIGN A RT D IRECTOR/D ESIGNER/I LLUSTRATOR: JOHN SAYLES C OUNTRY: USA I NDUSTRY/P URPOSE: COLLEGE – HÖHERE SCHULE – ETABLISSEMENT D'ENSEIGNE-MENT SUPÉRIEUR ■ **2** C LIENT: CALIFORNIA CENTER FOR THE ARTS D ESIGN F IRM: MIRES DESIGN, INC. A RT D IRECTOR/D ESIGNER: JOHN BALL C OUNTRY: USA I NDUSTRY/P URPOSE: VISUAL AND PERFORMING ARTS CENTER – ZENTRUM FÜR VISUELLE UND DARSTELLENDE KÜNSTE – CENTRE D'ARTS VISUELS ET D'ARTS DE REPRÉSENTATION ■ **3** C LIENT: AUSTRALIA UNIVERSITY D ESIGN F IRM: SWIETER DESIGN UNITED STATES A RT

1

D IRECTOR: JOHN SWIETER D ESIGNER: JOHN SWIETER C OUNTRY: USA I NDUSTRY/P URPOSE: UNIVERSITY – UNIVERSITÄT – UNIVERSITÉ ■ **4** C LIENT: DALLAS REHABILITATION CENTER D ESIGN F IRM: SWIETER DESIGN UNITED STATES A RT D IRECTOR: JOHN SWIETER D ESIGNER: PAUL MUNSTERMAN C OUNTRY: USA I NDUSTRY/P URPOSE: REHABILITATION CENTER – REHABILITATIONSZENTRUM – CENTRE DE RÉHABILITATION ■ **5** C LIENT: UNIVERSITY OF MINNESOTA, I.T.V. D ESIGN F IRM: BRAD NORR DESIGN D ESIGNER: BRAD NORR C OUNTRY: USA I NDUSTRY/P URPOSE: INTERACTIVE TELEVISION – INTERAKTIVES FERNSEHEN – TÉLÉVISION INTERACTIVE

2

3

4

5

1

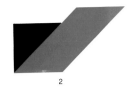

2

3

4

5

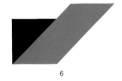

6

7

8

9

10

11

12

1 Client: HUNTER'S CREEK MIDDLE SCHOOL Design Firm: GRAPHICLEE Designer/Illustrator: LEE MORGAN Country: USA Industry/Purpose: PUBLIC SCHOOL – ÖFFENTLICHE SCHULE – ÉCOLE PUBLIQUE ■ **2**, **4–6** Client: PREFECTUAL UNIVERSITY OF KUMAMOTO Design Firm: NIPPON DESIGN CENTER, INC. Art Director/Designer: KAZUMASA NAGAI Country: JAPAN Industry/Purpose: UNIVERSITY – UNIVERSITÄT – UNIVERSITÉ ■ **3** Client: HUNTER'S CREEK ELEMENTARY SCHOOL Design Firm: GRAPHICLEE Designer: Illustrator: LEE MORGAN Country: USA Industry/Purpose: SCHOOL – SCHULE – ÉCOLE ■ **7** Client: JAMES MADISON UNIVERSITY Design Firm: SERAN DESIGN Art Director/Designer: SANG YOON Country: USA Industry/Purpose: UNIVERSITY – UNIVERSITÄT – UNIVERSITÉ ■ **8** Client: DE ANZA COLLEGE Design Firm: COLE STUDIO Art Director/Designer: MICHAEL COLE Country: USA Industry/Purpose: ELECTRONIC

13

PUBLISHING PROGRAM – ELEKTRONISCHES VERLAGSPROGRAMM – PROGRAMME D'ÉDITION ÉLECTRONIQUE ■ **9** Client: JAMES MADISON UNIVERSITY Design Firm: TRUDY COLE-ZIELANSKI DESIGN Art Director: Designer/Illustrator: TRUDY COLE-ZIELANSKI Country: USA Industry/Purpose: UNIVERSITY – UNIVERSITÄT – UNIVERSITÉ ■ **10–12** Client: MINISTERIUM FÜR WISSENSCHAFT UND KULTUR Design Firm: SIMON & SIMON Art Director: HELMUT SIMON Designers: HELMUT SIMON, ELFI SIMON Country: GERMANY Industry/Purpose: MINISTRY FOR SCIENCE, EDUCATION, AND CULTURE – MINISTERIUM FÜR WISSENSCHAFT, BILDUNG UND KULTUR – MINISTÈRE DES SCIENCES, DE L'EDUCATION ET DE LA CULTURE ■ **13** Client: DALLAS INSTITUTE OF VOCAL ARTS Design Firm: JOSEPH RATTAN DESIGN Art Director: JOSEPH RATTAN Designer: JOSEPH RATTAN Country: USA Industry/Purpose: INSTITUTE OF VOCAL ARTS – GESANGSSCHULE – ECOLE DE CHANT

2

3

4

1 Client: CALIFORNIA CENTER FOR THE ARTS MUSEUM Design Firm: MIRES DESIGN, INC. Art Director: JOHN BALL Designer: JOHN BALL Country: USA Purpose: VISUAL AND PERFORMING ARTS CENTER, MUSEUM EXHIBITION – ZENTRUM FÜR VISUELLE UND DARSTELLENDE KÜNSTE, MUSEUMSAUSSTELLUNG – CENTRE D'ARTS VISUELS ET D'ARTS DE REPRÉSENTATION, EXPOSITION AU MUSÉE D'ART ■ **2–4** Client: NEWMEDIA MAGAZINE Design Firm: CRONAN DESIGN, INC. Art Director: MICHAEL CRONAN Designers: MICHAEL CRONAN, LISA VAN ZANDT, MARIE GOODMAN DRECHSEL Illustrators: MICHAEL CRONAN, LISA VAN ZANDT Country: USA Purpose: EVENT – VERANSTALTUNG – MANIFESTATIONS

1

2

3

4

5

6

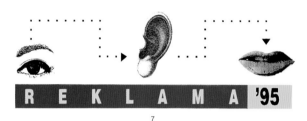

7

8

9

10

11

12

13

1 CLIENT: LJUBLJANSKI SEJEM DESIGN FIRM: KROG ART DIRECTOR/DESIGNER: EDI BERK COUNTRY: SLOVENIA PURPOSE: ARTS ANTIQUITIES FAIR – ANTIQUITÄTENMESSE – FOIRE 'ANTIQUITÉS ■ 2 CLIENT: CONCERTS FOR THE ENVIRONMENT DESIGN FIRM: CHARLES S. ANDERSON DESIGN COMPANY ART DIRECTOR: CHARLES S. ANDERSON DESIGNERS: CHARLES S. ANDERSON, JOEL TEMPLIN COUNTRY: USA PURPOSE: CONCERT – KONZERT ■ 3 CLIENT: LJUBLJANSKI SEJEM DESIGN FIRM: KROG ART DIRECTOR/DESIGNER: EDI BERK COUNTRY: SLOVENIA PURPOSE: AUTOMOBILE EXHIBITION – AUTOAUSSTELLUNG – EXPOSITION D'AUTOMOBILES ■ 4 CLIENT: SKY'S THE LIMIT DESIGN FIRM: ANTISTA FAIRCLOUGH DESIGN ART DIRECTORS/DESIGNERS: TOM ANTISTA, THOMAS FAIRCLOUGH COUNTRY: USA PURPOSE: SPECIALIZED PROMOTIONAL EVENTS COORDINATOR INCORPORATING FIREWORKS, LASERS, ETC. – ORGANISATOR SPEZIELLER VERANSTALTUNGEN EINSCHLIESSLICH FEUERWERK, LASERSHOWS ETC. – ORGANISATION DE MANIFESTATIONS (FEUX D'ARTIFICE, SPECTACLES LASER) ■ 5 CLIENT: STATE PRESERVATION BOARD DESIGN FIRM: SIBLEY/PETEET DESIGN, INC. ART DIRECTOR: REX PETEET DESIGNERS: REX PETEET, DEREK WELCH ILLUSTRATOR: DEREK WELCH COUNTRY: USA PURPOSE: TEXAS CAPITOL RESTORATION CELEBRATION – FEIER ANLÄSSLICH DER RESTAURIERUNG DES KAPITOLS VON TEXAS – FÊTE DONNÉE À L'OCCASION DE LA RÉNOVATION DU CAPITOLE, TEXAS ■ 6 CLIENT: FROM ALL WALKS OF LIFE ART DIRECTORS: ALICE DRUEDING, NICHOLAS ROOK DESIGNER/ILLUSTRATOR: LANCE RUSOFF COUNTRY: USA PURPOSE: AIDS AWARENESS – AIDS-AUFKLÄRUNG – CAMPAGNE D'INFORMATION SUR LE SIDA ■ 7 CLIENT: LITHUANIAN CENTER OF EXHIBITIONS DESIGN FIRM: "LUKRECIJA" ART DIRECTOR/DESIGNER: GIEDRE LISAUSKAITE COUNTRY: LITHUANIA PURPOSE: EXHIBITION CENTER – AUSSTELLUNGSZENTRUM – CENTRE D'EX-

14

POSITIONS ■ 8 CLIENT: CONCERTS FOR THE ENVIRONMENT DESIGN FIRM: CHARLES S. ANDERSON DESIGN COMPANY ART DIRECTOR: CHARLES S. ANDERSON DESIGNERS: CHARLES S. ANDERSON, TODD HAUSWIRTH ILLUSTRATORS: CHARLES S. ANDERSON, LYNN SCHULTE COUNTRY: USA PURPOSE: CONCERTS – KONZERTE ■ 9 CLIENT: MNP ART DIRECTOR/DESIGNER: MATTHIAS MENCKE COUNTRY: GERMANY PURPOSE: COMPANY FOR NEW COMMUNICATION AT SPORTS EVENTS AND ON TELEVISION – GESELLSCHAFT FÜR NEUE KOMMUNIKATION IM BEREICH SPORTVERANSTALTUNGEN UND TV – ENTREPRISE POUR UNE NOUVELLE COMMUNICATION DANS LE DOMAINE DES MANIFESTATIONS SPORTIVES ET DE LA TÉLÉVISION ■ 10 CLIENT: TEXAS SPECIAL OLYMPICS DESIGN FIRM: SIBLEY/PETEET DESIGN, INC. DESIGNERS: DEREK WELCH, JOHN EVANS ILLUSTRATOR: DEREK WELCH COUNTRY: USA PURPOSE: TEXAS SPECIAL OLYMPICS 1995 SUMMER GAMES – DIE SPEZIELLEN OLYMPISCHEN SOMMERSPIELE 1995 IN TEXAS – LES JEUX OLYMPIQUES SPÉCIAUX D'ÉTÉ 1995 AU TEXAS. ■ 11 CLIENT: LJUBLJANSKI SEJEM DESIGN FIRM: KROG ART DIRECTOR/DESIGNER: EDI BERK COUNTRY: SLOVENIA PURPOSE: NATURE AND HEALTH FAIR – NATURPRODUKT- UND GESUNDHEITSMESSE – SALON DES PRODUITS NATURELS ET DE LA SANTÉ ■ 12 CLIENT: BANZAI SPOKE-N-SKI DESIGN FIRM: MCCULLOUGH CREATIVE RESOURCES, INC. ART DIRECTOR/DESIGNER: MICHAEL SCHMALZ COUNTRY: USA PURPOSE: MOUNTAIN BIKE RACE – MOUNTAIN BIKE RENNEN – COURSE DE VTT ■ 13 CLIENTS: VICTORY GALLOP, KIM BALAJ DESIGN FIRM: BABCOCK & SCHMID ASSOCIATES, INC. COUNTRY: USA PURPOSE: CHARITY EVENT – WOHLTÄTIGKEITSVERANSTALTUNG – ŒUVRE DE CHARITÉ ■ 14 CLIENT: COMPAÑÍA DE ACTOS SINGULARES DESIGN FIRM: COSMIC ART DIRECTOR: JUAN DAVILA DESIGNERS: JUAN DAVILA, LAURA MESEGUER ILLUSTRATOR: CURRO COUNTRY: SPAIN PURPOSE: SPECIAL EVENTS ORGANIZATION – ORGANISATION SPEZIELLER ANLÄSSE – ORGANISATION DE MANIFESTATIONS

1

1 CLIENT: MINNESOTA ZOO DESIGN FIRM: RAPP COLLINS COMMUNICATIONS ART DIRECTOR: BRUCE EDWARDS DESIGNER/ILLUSTRATOR: BRUCE EDWARDS COUNTRY: USA INDUSTRY/PURPOSE: SUMMER EXHIBITION ON BUGS – SOMMERAUSSTELLUNG ÜBER KÄFER – EXPOSITION DE COLÉOPTÈRES ■ 2 CLIENT: AMERIFEST DALLAS DESIGN FIRM: RBMM/THE RICHARDS GROUP ART DIRECTOR/DESIGNER: HORACIO COBOS ILLUSTRATORS: HORACIO COBOS, WAYNE JOHNSON COUNTRY: USA INDUSTRY/PURPOSE: STREET FESTIVAL – STRASSENFEST – FESTIVAL DE RUE

1 Client: NIKE, INC. Design Firm: MIRES DESIGN Art Director/Designer: JOSÉ SERRANO Illustrator: TRACY SABIN Country: USA Industry: AN ALL-TURF SHOE – EIN SCHUH FÜR JEDES GELÄNDE – LA CHAUSSURE TOUT-TERRAIN ■ **2, 4** Client: FORRESTER'S Design Firm: ROOD MORT DESIGN Art Directors/ Designers: DON ROOD, PAUL MORT Illustrator: PAUL MORT Country: USA Industry: PERFORMANCE OUTERWEAR FOR GOLFERS –

1

ALLWETTERKLEIDUNG FÜR GOLFSPIELER – VÊTEMENTS POUR GOLFEURS ■ **3** Client: FRINGE HAIR STUDIO Design Firm: PLANET DESIGN COMPANY Art Director: KEVIN WADE, DANA LYTLE Designer: KEVIN WADE Country: USA Business: HAIR SALON – COIFFEUR-SALON – SALON DE COIFFURE ■ **5** Client: NIKE, INC. Design Firm: NIKE DESIGN Art Director/Designer: GUIDO BROUWERS Country: USA Industry/Purpose: LIMITED EDITION POSTER CARDS – PLAKATE IN POSTKARTENGRÖSSE – AFFICHES DE FORMAT CARTES POSTALES

2

FRINGE HAIR STUDIO

3

4

5

1 Client: MAXI MODO Design Firm: JAY VIGON STUDIO Art Director/Designer/Illustrator: JAY VIGON Country: USA Business: SPORTSWEAR STORE AND CLOTHING LINE – SPORTBEKLEIDUNGSLADEN UND KLEIDERMARKE – MAGASIN DE VÊTEMENTS DE SPORT ET LIGNE DE VÊTEMENTS ■ **2** Client: STRIDE RITE CORP. Design Firm: MORLA DESIGN Art Director: JENNIFER MORLA Designers: JENNIFER MORLA, CRAIG BAILEY Country: USA Industry: SHOE MANUFACTURER – SCHUHHERSTELLER – FABRICANT DE CHAUSSURES ■ **3** Client: GENTNER-KLEIDUNG GMBH Design Firm: DESIGN HOCH DREI Art Directors: SUSANNE WACKER, WOLFRAM SCHÄFFER Designer: DIETHARD KEPPLER Country: GERMANY Industry: TEXTILE RETAIL – TEXTIL-EINZELHANDEL – VENTE DE TEXTILE AU DÉTAIL ■ **4** Client: FACTOR PRODUKT MÜNCHEN – BOGNER MENS-WEAR Design Firm: FACTOR DESIGN Art Director/Designer/Illustrator: RÜDIGER GÖTZ Country: GERMANY Industry: MENSWEAR – HERRENBEKLEIDUNG – CONFECTION POUR HOMMES ■ **5** Client: QINDAO TRI-GENTS CLOTHING CO., LTD. Design Firm: CID LAB. INC. Art Director/Designer: YUKICHI TAKADA Agency: NIPPON INTERNATIONAL AGENCY Country: JAPAN Industry: FASHION INDUSTRY FOR MEN – HERRENBEKLEIDUNG – CONFECTION POUR HOMMES ■ **6** Client: DREAMMAKER CUSTOMS Design Firm: MIRES DESIGN, INC. Art Director/Designer: JOSÉ SERRANO Illustrator: TRACY SABIN Country: USA Industry: STREETWEAR CLOTH-ING LINE – MARKE FÜR STRASSENKLEIDUNG – LIGNE DE STREET WEAR ■ **7** Client: A.C. PIMENTA Design Firm: ANTERO FERREIRA DESIGN Art Director: ANTERO FERREIRA Designer/Illustrator: EDUARDO SOTTO MAYOR Country: PORTUGAL Industry: CHILDREN'S CLOTHING – KINDERKLEIDUNG – CONFECTION POUR ENFANTS ■ **8** Client: LEVI STRAUSS & CO. Design Firm: STONE YAMASHITA Art Directors: ROBERT STONE, KEITH

1

YAMASHITA Designer: MICHAEL BRALEY Country: USA Industry: CLOTHING MANUFACTURER – KLEIDERHER-STELLER – FABRICANT DE VÊTEMENTS ■ **9** Client: KOLON INTERNATIONAL CORP. Design Firm: DOOKIM DESIGN Art Director: DOO. H. KIM Designers: DONGIL LEE, SEUNGHEE LEE Industry: SPORTSWEAR MANU-FACTURER – SPORTBEKLEIDUNGSHERSTELLER – FABRICANT DE VÊTEMENTS DE SPORT ■ **10** Client: NATURAL NYLON/LORTEX Design Firm: PLANET DESIGN COMPANY Art Directors: KEVIN WADE, DANA LYTLE Designers: KEVIN WADE, MARTHA GRAETTINGER Country: USA Industry: FABRIC DESIGN – STOFF-DESIGN – DESIGN DE TISSUS ■ **11** Client: HAUBENEDER Design Firm: MOTTER-DESIGN Designer: OTHMAR MOTTER Country: AUSTRIA Industry: FASHION STORE FOR WOMEN, MEN AND CHILDREN – BEKLEIDUNGSHAUS FÜR DAMEN-, HERREN- UND KINDERMODE – CONFECTION POUR FEMMES, HOMMES ET ENFANTS ■ **12** Client: KRENHOLM Design Firm: VAAL DESIGN Art Director/Designer/Illustrator: IVAR SAKK Country: ESTONIA Industry: TEXTILE COMPANY – STOFFABRIKANT – FABRICANT DE TISSUS ■ **13** Client: CRAB'S KNITWEAR Design Firm: VALÖR TASARIM Art Director/Designer: SAVAS CEKIC Country: TURKEY Industry: FASHION BOUTIQUE FOR KNITWEAR – BOUTIQUE FÜR STRICKMODE – BOUTIQUE DE MODE MAILLE ET TRICOTS ■ **14** Client: HEAVEN Design Firm: HIRANO DESIGN GROUP Designers: NOBUO HIRANO, RURIKO KINJO Country: USA Industry: FASHION & SPORTS – MODE & SPORT ■ **15** Client: CARLETON/CHRIS HAIR & BODY Design Firm: LATITUDE/THE RICHARDS GROUP Art Director: FELIX P. SOCKWELL Country: USA Business: HAIR AND BODY SALON – HAAR-UND KÖRPERPFLEGE-SALON – SALON DE COIFFURE ET DE BEAUTÉ ■ **16** Client: CHUMS Design Firm: CHARLES S. ANDERSON DESIGN COMPANY Art Director: CHARLES S. ANDERSON Designer: TODD PIPER-HAUSWIRTH Country: USA Industry: CLOTHING MANUFACTURING – KLEIDERHERSTELLER – FABRICANT DE VÊTEMENTS

2

3

4

5

6

7

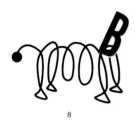

8

9

10

11

12

13

14

15

16

(LOGOS THIS SPREAD) **1–7** CLIENT: TSUKAMOTO CO., LTD. DESIGN FIRM: SHIGEO KATSUOKA DESIGN STUDIO
ART DIRECTOR: SHIGEO KATSUOKA DESIGNERS: SHIGEO KATSUOKA, AKIKO SHIMAZU COUNTRY: JAPAN
INDUSTRY: APPAREL MARKETING COMPANY — BEKLEIDUNGSGROSSHANDEL — FABRICANT DE VÊTEMENTS

1

2

3

4

5

1 Client: TEE SHIRT COMPANY Design Firm: MIRES DESIGN, INC. Art Director/Designer: JOSÉ SERRANO Country: USA Industry/Purpose: T-SHIRT MANUFACTURER – T-SHIRT-HERSTELLER – FABRICANT DE T-SHIRTS ■ **2** Client: JANTZEN, INC. Design Firm: PRINCIPIA GRAPHICA Art Directors: ROBIN RICKABAUGH, HEIDI RICKABAUGH Designers: KIMBERLY LEW, ROBIN RICKABAUGH Country: USA Industry/Purpose: CLOTHING MANUFACTURER – KLEIDERHERSTELLER – FABRICANT DE VÊTEMENTS ■ **3** Client: K2 JAPAN Design Firm: MODERN DOG Art Director/Designer/Illustrator: MICHAEL STRASSBURGER Country: JAPAN Industry: SKIS

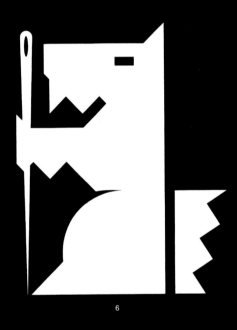

6

■ **4** Client: PALM SPRINGS Design Firm: MIRES DESIGN, INC. Art Director/Designer: JOSÉ SERRANO Country: USA Industry/Purpose: T-SHIRT FOR SPRING BREAK – T-SHIRT FÜR FRÜHJAHRSFERIEN – T-SHIRTS ■ **5** Client: LA GEAR Design Firm: MIRES DESIGN, INC. Art Director/Designer: SCOTT MIRES Illustrator: TRACY SABIN Country: USA Industry/Purpose: FITNESS APPAREL – SPORTKLEIDUNG – VÊTEMENTS DE SPORT ■ **6** Client: SCOTLAND YARDS FABRICS AND INTERIORS Design Firm: SIBLEY/PETEET DESIGN, INC. Art Director/Designer: REX PETEET Illustrator: REX PETEET Country: USA Industry/Purpose: INTERIOR FABRICS AND FURNITURE – INNENDEKORATION UND MÖBEL – MEUBLES ET DÉCORATION D'INTÉRIEUR

1

2

3

4

5

1 CLIENT: TELEWORKS DESIGN FIRM: RHODES STAFFORD WINES ART DIRECTORS: BRAD WINES, ANDREW ROTH DESIGNER/ILLUSTRATOR: ANDREW ROTH COUNTRY: USA INDUSTRY: FILM PRODUCTION COMPANY – FILMPRODUK-TIONSGESELLSCHAFT – SOCIÉTÉ DE PRODUCTION CINÉMATOGRAPHIQUE ■ 2 CLIENT: TWENTIETH TELEVISION DESIGN FIRM: WHITE PLUS... ART DIRECTOR: TRINA NUOVO DESIGNER: DAVIS HENRY COUNTRY: USA INDUSTRY: ENTERTAINMENT – UNTERHALTUNG – DIVERTISSEMENTS ■ 3 CLIENT: GOLDEN HARVEST FILMS DESIGN FIRM: PPA DESIGN LTD. ART DIRECTOR/DESIGNER: BYRON JACOBS COUNTRY: HONG KONG INDUSTRY: DISTRIBUTOR OF ASIAN FILMS TO NORTH AMERICA – VERLEIH ASIATISCHER FILME IN NORDAMERIKA – DISTRIBUTION DE FILMS ASIA-

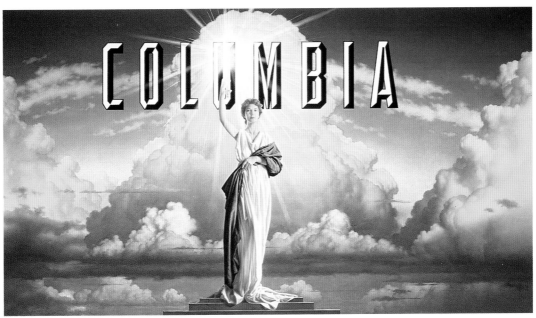

6

TIQUES EN AMÉRIQUE DU NORD ■ 4 CLIENT: DEBMAR STUDIOS DESIGN FIRM: WHITE PLUS... ART DIRECTOR: TRINA NUOVO DESIGNER: VICTORIA BERRY ILLUSTRATOR: WILL NELSON COUNTRY: USA INDUSTRY: ENTERTAINMENT, MOVIE DISTRIBUTOR – UNTERHALTUNG, FILMVERLEIH ■ 5 CLIENT: FIELD TRIP PRODUCTIONS DESIGN FIRM: SIBLEY/ PETEET DESIGN, INC. ART DIRECTOR: REX PETEET DESIGNERS: REX PETEET, DEREK WELCH ILLUSTRATOR: DEREK WELCH COUNTRY: USA INDUSTRY: CHILDREN'S EDUCATIONAL VIDEO PRODUCTION – VIDEO-BILDUNGSPROGRAMME FÜR KINDER ■ 6 CLIENT: COLUMBIA PICTURES DESIGN FIRM: THE MEDNICK GROUP ART DIRECTOR/DESIGNER: SCOTT MEDNICK ILLUSTRATOR: MICHAEL DEAS COUNTRY: USA INDUSTRY: FILM PRODUCTION – FILMPRODUKTION

1 Client: TIMES 3 PRODUCTIONS Design Firm: GEER DESIGN, INC. Art Director: MARK GEER Designers: MARK GEER, HEIDI FLYNN ALLEN Country: USA Industry/Purpose: FILM PRODUCTION – FILMPRODUKTION ■ **2–4, 12** Client: TURNER ENTERTAIMENT Design Firm: CHARLES S. ANDERSON DESIGN COMPANY Art Director: CHARLES S. ANDERSON Designers: CHARLES S. ANDERSON, PAUL HOWALT, JOEL TEMPLIN Country: USA Industry/Purpose: ENTERTAINMENT CONGLOMERATE – UNTERHALTUNGS-KONGLOMERAT ■ **5** Client: SPOT WELDERS Design Firm: JAY VIGON STUDIO Art Director/Designer: JAY VIGON Co-Designer/Producer: CAROLINE PLASENCIA Printer: DESIGN SOURCE Country: USA Industry/Purpose: FILM PRODUCTION – FILMPRODUKTION ■ **6** Client: KINOS AARAU Design Firm: WILD & FREY Art Director: HEINZ WILD Designer: HEINZ WILD Country: SWITZERLAND Industry/Purpose: MOVIE THEATER – KINO ■ **7** Client: KINOVERWALTUNG ATELIER & LUPE Designer: ISABELLE DEVAUX Country: GERMANY Industry/Purpose:

1

CINEMA ADMINISTRATION – KINOVERWALTUNG ■ **8** Client: ATOMIC PICTURES Design Firm: SAYLES GRAPHIC DESIGN Art Director: JOHN SAYLES Designer: JOHN SAYLES Illustrator: JOHN SAYLES Country: USA Industry/Purpose: AUDIO VISUAL ■ **9** Client: MARY CARBINE Design Firm: 4TH PRIMARY Art Directors/Designers: JOHN MARIN, MICHÉLE-HOAIDUC NGUYEN Country: USA Industry/Purpose: FREELANCE FILM PRODUCER – FREIE FILMPRODUZENTIN ■ **10** Client: FIREDOG PICTURES Design Firm: LISA LEVIN DESIGN Art Director/Designer: LISA LEVIN Illustrator: MICHAEL SCHWAB Country: USA Industry/Purpose: CHILDREN'S VIDEO PRODUCTION – VIDEO-PRODUKTIONEN FÜR KINDER ■ **11** Client: GRANITE CITY PRODUCTIONS Design Firm: RBMM/THE RICHARDS GROUP Designer: LUIS D. ACEVEDO Country: USA Industry/Purpose: PRODUCTION COMPANY ■ **13** Client: BAD DOG PICTURES Design Firm: KILFOY DESIGN Designer: MICHAEL KILFOY Photographer: TOM PETRI Country: USA Industry/Purpose: FILM, VIDEO

2

3

4

5

6

7

8

9

10

11

12

13

1, 2 CLIENT: PHOENIX CAPITAL MANAGEMENT LTD. DESIGN FIRM: PPA DESIGN LTD. ART DIRECTOR/DESIGNER: BYRON JACOBS COUNTRY: HONG KONG INDUSTRY/PURPOSE: FINANCIAL MANAGEMENT CONSULTANT — FINANZ-BERATER ■ 3, 5 CLIENT: MULTIVALORES GRUPO FINANCIERO DESIGN FIRM/ART DIRECTOR/DESIGNER: POINT ZERO DESIGN COUNTRY: MEXICO INDUSTRY/PURPOSE: FINANCIAL INSTITUTION — FINANZINSTITUT ■ 4 CLIENT:

1

FINANCIAL ARCHITECTS, INC. DESIGN FIRM: KIRBY STEPHENS DESIGN, INC. ART DIRECTOR: KIRBY STEPHENS DESIGNERS: KIRBY STEPHENS, BILL JONES COUNTRY: USA INDUSTRY/PURPOSE: FINANCIAL PLANNER — FINANZ-BERATER ■ 6 CLIENT: HUNTINGTON BANKS DESIGN FIRM: RICKABAUGH GRAPHICS ART DIRECTOR: ERIC RICKABAUGH DESIGNER: ERIC RICKABAUGH ARTIST: TONY MEUSER COUNTRY: USA INDUSTRY/PURPOSE: BANKING —

2

3

4

5

6

1 Client: U.S.—ARAB CHAMBER OF COMMERCE Design Firm: GUNN ASSOCIATES Art Director/Illustrator: MICHAEL BEAGAN Designer: DAVID SCHWENDEMAN Country: USA Industry: CHAMBER OF COMMERCE — HANDELSKAMMER ■ 2 Client: FIRST CHICAGO BANK Design Firm: WECHSLER & PARTNERS, INC. Art Director: KAREN KNORR Designer: MICHAEL ROMAN, ANNETTA VON BRANDIS Illustrator: MICHAEL BULL Country: USA Industry: BANKING — BANK — BANQUE ■ 3 Client: LAIDLAW & CO. Design Firm/Designer: KELLY CAVENER Country: USA Industry: INVESTMENT COMPANY — ANLAGEBERATER ■ 4 Client: IDBI BANK LTD. Design Firm: GRAPHIC COMMUNICATION CONCEPTS Art Director/Designer: SUDARSHAN DHEER Country: INDIA Industry: BANKING — BANK — BANQUE ■ 5 Client: LJUBLJANSKA BANKA Art Director/Designer/Illustrator: MARJANA BIZILJ Country: SLOVENIA Industry: BANKING — BANK — BANQUE ■ 6 Client: CREDITO

1

2

3

4

5

6

7

8

9

INDUSTRIALE SARDO Design Firm: MOTTER-DESIGN Designer: OTHMAR MOTTER Country: ITALY Industry: PRIVATBANK — PRIVATBANK — BANQUE PRIVÉ ■ 7 Client: BTV Design Firm: MOTTER-DESIGN Designer: OTHMAR MOTTER Country: AUSTRIA Industry: BANKING — BANK — BANQUE ■ 8 Client: STEWART ISAACSON, Designer: PHILIP QUINN Country: USA Industry: INVESTMENT ADVISORY SERVICES — ANLAGEBERATER ■ 9 Client: FINNISH OPTIONS EXCHANGE Design Firm: METSÄRANTA ART & DESIGN Art Director/Designer: ANTTI METSÄRANTA Country: FINLAND Industry: OPTIONS EXCHANGE FINANCIAL SERVICES — ANLAGEBERATER ■ 10 Client: ICICI BANK Design Firm: GRAPHIC COMMUNICATION CONCEPTS Art Director/Designer: SUDARSHAN DHEER Country: INDIA Industry: BANKING — BANK — BANQUE ■ 11 Client: FIRST NATIONAL BANK SOUTH AFRICA Design Firm: TRADEMARK DESIGN (PTY) LTD. Art Director: CLIVE H. GAY Designers: CLIVE H. GAY, DARREN GAY, CRAIG LYON Country: SOUTH AFRICA Industry: BANKING — BANK — BANQUE

10

11

1

2

3

4

5

1 Client: CITY OF OAKLAND Design Firm: STEVEN LEE DESIGN Art Director/Designer/Illustrator: STEVEN LEE Country: USA Description: CITY GOVERNMENT – STADTVERWALTUNG ■ **2** Client: NIIGATA PREFECTURE Design Firm: NIPPON DESIGN CENTER, INC. Art Director/Designer: KAZUMASA NAGAI Country: JAPAN Description: GOVERNMENT – REGIERUNG ■ **3** Client: MINISTRY OF ENVIRONMENT Art Director/Designer: STEFAN TCHAKAROV Country: BULGARIA Description: MINISTRY OF ENVIRONMENT – UMWELTMINISTERIUM ■ **4** Client: ÖSTERREICHISCHES AUSSENMINISTERIUM Design Firm: ATELIER LOTHAR ÄMILIAN HEINZLE Art

6

Director: LOTHAR ÄMILIAN HEINZLE Designer: LOTHAR ÄMILIAN HEINZLE Country: AUSTRIA Description: AUSTRIAN FOREIGN OFFICE – AUSSENMINISTERIUM – MINISTÈRE DES AFFAIRES ÉTRANGÈRES ■ **5** Client: STATE ENTERPRISE PORT OF TALLINN Art Director/Designer: MARGUS HAAVAMÄGI Country: ESTONIA Description: PORT OF TALLINN – HAFENBEHÖRDE – ENTREPRISE D'ÉTAT PORT DE TALLINN ■ **6** Client: KAWASAKI CITY Design Firm: KEISUKE UNOSAWA DESIGN Art Director/Designer: KEISUKE UNOSAWA Country: JAPAN Description: CITY GOVERNMENT – STADTVERWALTUNG – MUNICIPALITÉ DE KAWASAKI CITY

1 Client: CORAM HEALTHCARE Design Firm: RUNYAN HINSCHE ASSOCIATES Art Director: JIM BERTE Designers: MARIA DELOTTA, JIM BERTE Country: USA Description: HEALTHCARE – GESUNDHEITSWESEN – SANTÉ PUBLIQUE ■ **2** Client: OVID Design Firm: THE LEONHARDT GROUP Designers: DENNIS CLOUSE, RAY UENO Country: USA Description: ELECTRONIC MEDICAL INFORMATION RETRIEVAL SERVICES – ELEKTRONISCHE VERARBEITUNG MEDIZINISCHER INFORMATIONEN – TRAITEMENT ÉLECTRONIQUE DE DONNÉES MÉDICALES ■ **3** Client: ZENECA PHARMACEUTICALS Design Firm: NAYLOR, DEDONATO & WOLF Art Director: JIM PROKELL Designer: BILL HEALEY Illustrator: TOM BRILL Country: USA Industry: PHARMACEUTICAL COMPANY

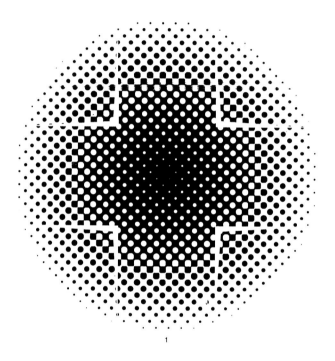

1

– PHARMA-UNTERNEHMEN – ENTREPRISE PHARMACEUTIQUE ■ **4** Client: WEST SOUND SPORTS THERAPY Design Firm: SWIETER DESIGN UNITED STATES Art Director: JOHN SWIETER Designers: JOHN SWIETER, JIM VOGEL Country: USA Description: PHYSICAL THERAPY CLINIC – KLINIK FÜR PHYSIOTHERAPIE – CLINIQUE DE PHYSIOTHÉRAPIE ■ **5** Client: THOMSEN DENTAL ASSOCIATES Design Firm: DOTZLER DESIGN Art Director/Designer: RAY DOTZLER Country: USA Description: DENTIST – ZAHNARZT – DENTISTE ■ **6** Client: VIRGINIA MASON GROUP HEALTH ALLIANCE Design Firm: SPANGLER ASSOCIATES Art Director/Designer/ Illustrator: MICHAEL CONNORS Country: USA Description: HEALTH CARE SERVICES – GESUNDHEITSWESEN – SANTÉ PUBLIQUE

O V I D

2

3

4

5

6

1 Client: NEW ENGLAND HOSPITAL MARKETING & PUBLIC RELATIONS ASSOC. Design Firm: POLLARD DESIGN Art Director/Designer: JEFF POLLARD Country: USA Description: HOSPITAL INDUSTRY AWARDS PROGRAM – PR FÜR SPITÄLER – RELATIONS PUBLIQUES POUR DES HÔPITAUX ■ 2 Client: EAGLE REHAB CORP. Design Firm: SWIETER DESIGN UNITED STATES Art Director: JOHN SWIETER Designer: MARK FORD Country: USA Description: PHYSICAL THERAPY MEDICAL CORPORATION – PHYSIOTHERAPIE – PHYSIOTHÉRAPIE ■ 3 Client: GLENCOE-MCGRAW-HILL Design Firm: MARS COMMUNICATIONS Art Director/Designer: TIMOTHY J RYAN Country: USA Description: BOOK PUBLISHING COMPANY – BUCHVERLAG – MAISON D'ÉDITION ■ 4 Client: LOIS COON Design Firm: POLLARD DESIGN Art Director/Designer: JEFF POLLARD Country: USA Description: PSYCHOTHERAPIST – PSYCHOTHERAPEUT – PSYCHOTHÉRAPEUTE ■ 5 Client: NEW MEDICAL AND SPECIAL TECHNOLOGY CENTRE Design Firm: LINIA GRAFIC Art Director/Designer/Illustrator: DMITRY DOLGOV Country: RUSSIA Description: MEDICAL CENTER – MEDIZINISCHES ZENTRUM – CENTRE MÉDICALE ■ 6 Client: ADVANCED CARDIOVASCULAR SYSTEMS Design Firm: MIRES DESIGN Art Director/Designer: SCOTT MIRES Country: USA Description: TRAVEL INCENTIVE – LEISTUNGSANSPORN FÜR VERTRETER – VOYAGES DE MOTIVATION POUR LES REPRÉSENTATNTS ■ 7 Client: SURGICAL SPECIALISTS Design Firm: BASLER DESIGN GROUP Art Director: BILL BASLER Designers: BILL BASLER, COLLEEN WENDLING, KOBE Country: USA Description: SURGERY – CHIRURGIE ■ 8 Client: METROCENTER CHIROPRACTIC P.A. Design Firm: ZAUHAR DESIGN Art

1

Director/Designer/Illustrator: DAVID ZAUHAR Country: USA Description: CHIROPRACTIC FIRM – CHIROPRAKTIKER CHIROPRATICIEN ■ 9 Client: "SISTERS OF MERCY" Art Director/Designer: IVICA BELINIC Illustrator: IVICA BELINIC Country: CROATIA Description: HOSPITAL – SPITAL – HÔPITAL ■ 10 Client: BROADLAWNS MEDICAL CENTER Design Firm: DESIGNGROUP Art Director/Designer: DAN ELLIS Illustrator: DAN ELLIS Country: USA Description: PSYCHIATRIC-MUSIC THERAPY – PSYCHIATRISCHE-MUSIKALISCHE THERAPIE – THÉRAPIE PAR LA MUSIQUE ■ 11 Client: MARYLAND EQUINE CENTER Design Firm: PETERSON DESIGN Designer: CHRISTOPHER PETERSON Country: USA Description: VETERINARY CLINIC FOR HORSES – PFERDEKLINIK – CLINIQUE VÉTÉRINAIRE POUR CHEVAUX ■ 12 Client: ̄ENATSVERWALTUNG FÜR GESUNDHEIT Art Director/Designer: HANS-GEORG GERASCH Country: GERMANY Description: SPORTS MEDICIN – SPORTMEDIZIN – MÉDECINE SPORTIVE ■ 13 Client: QUEEN MARY HOSPITAL Design Firm: ALAN CHAN DESIGN Art Director: ALAN CHAN YAU-KIN Designers: ALAN CHAN YAU-KIN, LIZ WATSON Illustrator: LIZ WATSON Country: HONG KONG Description: HOSPITAL – SPITAL – HÔPI-TAL ■ 14 Client: STADT-APOTHEKE DORNBIRN Design Firm: MOTTER-DESIGN Designer: OTHMAR MOTTER Country: AUSTRIA Description: PHARMACY – APOTHEKE – PHARMACIE ■ 15 Client: INTERNATIONAL HOSPITAL CORPORATION Design Firm: GIBBS BARONET Art Director/Designer: WILLIE BARONET Country: USA Description: HOSPITAL – SPITAL – HÔPITAL ■ 16 Client: KRANKENHAUS MARIA EBENE Design Firm: MOTTER-DESIGN Designer: OTHMAR MOTTER Country: AUSTRIA Description: HOSPITAL – SPITAL – HÔPITAL

2

3

4

5

6

7

8

9

10

11

12

13

14

15

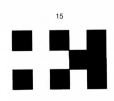

16

1

2

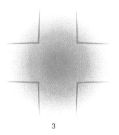

3

4

5

1 Client: TEXAS ORTHOPEDIC HOSPITAL Design Firm: PENNEBAKER DESIGN Art Director/Designer: HAESUN KIM LERCH Country: USA Description: HOSPITAL – SPITAL – HÔPITAL ■ **2** Client: PHILADELPHIA FERTILITY INSTITUTE Design Firm: ZEEWY DESIGN Art Director: ORLY ZEEWY Designer: LIA CALHOUN Country: USA Description: MEDICAL PRACTICE – ARZTPRAXIS – CABINET MÉDICAL ■ **3** Client: CORAM HEALTHCARE Design Firm: POINT ZERO Art Direction/Design: POINT ZERO Country: USA Description: HEALTHCARE COMPANY – KRANKENKASSE – CAISSE-MALADIES ■ **4** Client: FRITZ HILLE Design Firm: FANTASTIC NEW DESIGNMENT Art

6

Directors/Designers: MICHAEL RASCH, THOMAS LASS Country: GERMANY Description: OPTICIAN – OPTIKER – OPTICIEN ■ **5** Client: ADVENTIST HEALTH CARE MID-ATLANTIC Design Firm: SUPON DESIGN GROUP Creative Director: SUPON PHORNIRUNLIT, ANDREW DOLAN Designer: ANTHONY FLETCHER Country: USA Description: HEALTHCARE PROGRAM – GESUNDHEITSWESEN – PROGRAMME SANITAIRE ■ **6** Client: NATIONAL PHYSICIANS NETWORK Design Firm: ANTISTA FAIRCLOUGH DESIGN Art Directors/Designers: TOM ANTISTA, THOMAS FAIRCLOUGH Country: USA Description: PHYSICIAN AND HOSPITAL NETWORKER – NETZ- WERK VON ÄRZTEN UND SPITALPFLEGEPERSONAL – RÉSEAU DE MÉDECINS ET DE PERSONNEL SOIGNANT

1

see

2

3

4

5

1 Client: PACE Design Firm: DENNARD CREATIVE Art Director/Illustrator: BOB DENNARD Designers: BOB DENNARD, CHRIS WOOD Country: USA Industry/Purpose: GROUP PROMOTING THE ARTS – KUNSTFÖRDERUNG – PROMOTION ARTISTIQUE ■ **2** Client: THE FRIENDS OF PHOTOGRAPHY Design Firm: TOKI DESIGN Art Directors: MICHIKO TOKI, MICHAEL READ Designer: MICHIKO TOKI Country: USA Industry/Purpose: GROUP OF PHOTOGRAPHY ENTHUSIASTS – VEREIN VON PHOTOLIEBHABERN – ASSOCIATION DES ADEPTES DE LA PHOTOGRAPHIE ■ **3** Client: UZAY ÖRGÜ YÜNLERI Design Firm: 3. KUSAK ILETISIM HIZMETLERI A.S. Art Director/Designer: MEHMET ALI TÜRKMEN Country: TURKEY Industry/Purpose: WOOL SHOP – WOLLADEN – MAGASIN DE LAINE ■ **4** Client:

6

WOMEN'S NATIONAL BOOK ASSOCIATION Design Firm: PETERSON & COMPANY Art Director/Designer: NHAN T. PHAM Country: USA Industry/Purpose: BOOK ASSOCIATION – BUCHCLUB – CLUB DU LIVRE ■ **5** Client: CAGDAS SINEMA OYUNCULARI PERNEGI Design Firm: YOUNG & RUBICAM/REKLAMEVI Art Director/Designer/Illustrator: BÜLENT ERKMEN Country: TURKEY Industry: CONTEMPORARY FILM ARTIST'S ASSOCIATION – VERBAND ZEITGE-NÖSSISCHER FILMSCHAFFENDER – ASSOCIATION DE CINÉASTES CONTEMPORAINS ■ **6** Client: EXCHANGE PUBLISHING HOUSE Design Firm: SINO WEST DESIGN COMPANY Art Director/Designer: XU WANG Calligrapher: KAN TAI-KEUNG Photographer: KA-SING LEE Country: HONG KONG Industry: PUBLISHER – VERLAG – MAISON D'ÉDITION

1 Client: MENTAL HEALTH ASSOCIATION OF GREATER DALLAS Design Firm: SULLIVANPERKINS Art Director/ Designer: KELLY ALLEN Country: USA Description: PUBLIC HEALTH CARE – GESUNDSHEITSWESEN – SANTÉ PUBLIQUE ■ **2** Client: THE AMERICAN CANCER SOCIETY Design Firm: ROBIN SHEPHERD STUDIOS Art Director/Illustrator: JAMIE BORDERS Country: USA Description: NON-PROFIT ORGANIZATION – KREBSLIGA – LIGUE CONTRE LE CANCER ■ **3** Client: MINNESOTA TRIAL LAWYERS ASSOCIATION Design Firm: SCOTT THARES DESIGN Art Director/Designer/Illustrator: SCOTT THARES Country: USA Purpose: LAWYER'S ASSOCIATION – ANWALTSKAMMER – ORDRE DES AVOCATS ■ **4** Client: NATIONAL GREYHOUND ADOPTION PROGRAM Design Firm: STUDIO D DESIGN Art Director/Designer/Illustrator: LAURIE DEMARTINO Country: USA Description: NON-PROFIT ORGANIZATION – ADOPTION VON WINDHUNDE – PROGRAMME EN FAVEUR DES LÉVRIERS ■ **5** Client: BÜRGERSCHÜTZENVEREIN ST. ANTON Design Firm: STIEHL – OTTE GMBH, WERBEAGENTUR Art Director/Designer: THOMAS OTTE Country: GERMANY Description: SHOOTING CLUB – SCHÜTZENVEREIN – SOCIÉTÉ DE TIR ■ **6** Client: ATLANTA VISION IN DESIGN Design Firm: WAGES DESIGN Art Directors: BOB WAGES, TED FABELLA Designer: TED FABELLA Illustrator: KEVIN KEMMERLY Country: USA Description: CONSORTIUM OF DESIGNERS AND ARCHITECTS IN ATLANTA – KONSORTIUM VON DESIGNERN UND ARCHITEKTEN IN ATLANTA – CONSORTIUM DE DESIGNERS ET D'ARCHITECTES À ATLANTA ■ **7** Client: SOCIETY FOR ENVIRONMENTAL GRAPHIC DESIGN Design Firm: KEN SHAFER DESIGN Art Director/Designer/Illustrator: KEN SHAFER Country: USA Description: VISUAL COMMUNICATIONS – VERBAND FÜR GRAPHIK- DESIGN IM ÖFFENTLICHEN RAUM – ASSSOCIATION POUR LA PROMOTION DU DESIGN GRAPHIQUE DANS LES ESPACES PUBLICS ■ **8** Client: DESHUTES COUNTY COALITION FOR HUMAN DIGNITY Design Firm: PINK FISH GRAPHICS Art Director/Designer/Illustrator: STUART CRAIG Country: USA

1

Description: NON-PROFIT SOCIAL ACTION GROUP – VERBAND ZUM SCHUTZ DER MENSCHENWÜRDE – ASSOCIATION POUR LA DÉFENSE DE LA DIGNETÉ HUMAINE ■ **9** Client: ASSOCIATION OF HIGHER EDUCATION FACILITIES OFFICERS Design Firm: BREMMER & GORIS COMMUNICATIONS Art Director: DENNIS GORIS Designer/Illustrator: PETER BUTTECALI Country: USA Purpose: CONFERENCE OF EDUCATIONAL GROUPS – VERBAND VON HOCHSCHULLEHRERN – ASSOCIATION DES PROFESSEURS DE L'ENSEIGNEMENT SUPÉRIEUR ■ **10** Client: EDUCATIONAL LEADERSHIP CENTER Design Firm: GRAPHICLEE Designer/Illustrator: LEE MORGAN Country: USA Description: PUBLIC SCHOOL – ÖFFENTLICHE SCHULE – ECOLE PUBLIQUE ■ **11** Client: INDUSTRIAL DESIGN COUNCIL OF AUSTRALIA Design Firm: GRANT JORGENSEN GRAPHIC DESIGN Art Director/Designer: GRANT JORGENSEN Country: AUSTRALIA Purpose: INDUSTRIAL DESIGN AWARDS PROGRAM – PREIS FÜR INDUSTRIE-DESIGN – PRIX DE DESIGN INDUSTRIEL ■ **12** Client: COMBINED JEWISH PHILANTHROPIES Design Firm: GILL FISHMAN ASSOCIATES Art Director/Designer: GILL FISHMAN Illustrator: MARCIE SEAGER Country: USA Description: PHILANTHROPY – JÜDISCHER PHILANTROPISCHER VERBAND – ASSOCIATION PHILANTHROPIQUE JUIVE ■ **13** Client: RIVER VALLEY COMMUNITY CHURCH Design Firm: THE LARSON GROUP Art Director/Designer: SCOTT DVORAK Country: USA Description: CHURCH – KIRCHE – ÉGLISE ■ **14** Client: BEAVERDALE NEIGHBORHOOD ASSOCIATION Design Firm: SAYLES GRAPHIC DESIGN Art Director/Designer/Illustrator: JOHN SAYLES Country: USA Description: NEIGHBORHOOD/ ASSOCIATION – NACHBARSCHAFTSVEREIN – ASSOCIATION DE BON VOISINAGE ■ **15** Client: ZIPP-HAIRCUTTERS Design Firm: FACTOR DESIGN Art Director/Designer/Illustrator: RÜDIGER GÖTZ Country: GERMANY Description: HAIRCUTTER – SALONS DE COIFFURE ■ **16** Client: ASSOCIATED PRESS Design Firm: JENKINS & PAGE Art Director/Designer: JEFF JENKINS Country: USA Purpose: DIGITAL DELIVERY OF COMICS TO NEWSPAPERS – DIGITALE COMICS FÜR ZEITUNGEN – BANDES DESSINÉES DIGITALES POUR QUOTIDIENS

2

3

4

5

6

7

8

9

10

11

12

13

14

15

16

1 CLIENT: PLAYBOY MBF FOUNDATION DESIGN FIRM: VSA PARTNERS, INC. ART DIRECTOR: DANA ARNETT DESIGNER: MELISSA WATERS PHOTOGRAPHER: HOWARD BJORNSON COUNTRY: USA DESCRIPTION: AIDS FOUNDATION – AIDS-STIFTUNG – FONDATION POUR LA LUTTE CONTRE LE SIDA ■ 2 CLIENT: THE MOUNTAINEERS DESIGN FIRM: MICHAEL COURTNEY DESIGN ART DIRECTOR: MICHAEL COURTNEY DESIGNER: MICHAEL COURTNEY ILLUSTRATORS: MICHAEL COURTNEY, BRIAN O'NEILL COUNTRY: USA DESCRIPTION: RECREATION AND CONSERVATION ORGANIZA-

1

2

3

TION – NATURSCHUTZVERBAND – ASSOCIATION POUR LA PROTECTION DE LA NATURE ■ 3 CLIENT: HEAL THE BAY DESIGN FIRM: TEAM ONE ADVERTISING DESIGNER: GABRIELLE MAYEUR COUNTRY: USA DESCRIPTION: PUBLIC SERVICE ORGANIZATION – UMWELTSCHUTZORGANISATION – ASSOCIATION POUR LA PROTECTION DE L'ENVI-RONNEMENT ■ 4 CLIENT: THE GRAMMARIAN GROUP DESIGN FIRM: JOSEPH RATTAN DESIGN ART DIRECTOR: JOSEPH RATTAN DESIGNER: GREG MORGAN COUNTRY: USA DESCRIPTION: AUTHORS, EDITORS AND WRITERS ORGANIZA-TION – AUTOREN- UND JOURNALISTENVERBAND – ASSOCIATION D'AUTEURS, D'ÉDITEURS ET D'ÉCRIVAINS

g

4

1

2

3

4

5

EESTI
KUNSTNIKE

1 Client: THE SHORES Design Firm: BRAINSTORM INC. Art Director/Designer/Illustrator: KEN KOESTER Country: USA Description: RESIDENTIAL COMMUNITY – WOHNGEMEINDE – COMMUNAUTÉ RÉSIDENTIELLE ■ **2** Client: VORARLBERGER WOHN-UND SIEDLUNGSGESELLSCHAFT M.B.H. Design Firm: MOTTER-DESIGN Designer: OTHMAR MOTTER Country: AUSTRIA Description: REAL ESTATE COMPANY – IMMOBILIEN-GESELLSCHAFT – AGENCE IMMOBILIER ■ **3** Client: SAN FRANCISCO TUBA QUARTET Designer: PHILIP QUINN Country: USA Description: MUSICAL ORGANIZATION – MUSIKVERBAND – SOCIÉTÉ DE MUSIQUE ■ **4** Client: LAKEWOOD UNITED METHODIST CHURCH Design Firm: RBMM/ THE RICHARDS GROUP Art Director: BRIAN BOYD, WEBB BLEVIN Illustrator: WEBB BLEVIN Country: USA Description: COMMUNITY MEETING PLACE –

6

7

8

METHODISTEN-KIRCHE – EGLISE MÉTHODISTE ■ **5** Client: ESTONIAN ARTISTS' ASSOCIATION Art Director: MARGUS HAAVAMÄGI Designer: MARGUS HAAVAMÄGI Country: ESTONIA Description: ARTISTS' ASSOCIATION – KÜNSTLERVERBAND – ASSOCIATION D'ARTISTES ■ **6** Client: ÖSTERREICHISCHE RECHTSANWALTSKAMMER Design Firm: MOTTER-DESIGN Designer: OTHMAR MOTTER Country: AUSTRIA Description: LAWYERS' ASSOCIATION – ANWALTSKAMMER – ORDRE DES AVOCATS ■ **7** Client: HARLEY-DAVIDSON CLUB Design Firm: TINGUELY CONCEPT Designer: JOHANN TERRETTAZ Country: SWITZERLAND Description: MOTORCYCLE CLUB – MOTORRAD-CLUB – CLUB DE MOTARDS ■ **8** Client: 1995 SPECIAL OLYMPICS Design Firm: PETER GOOD GRAPHIC DESIGN Art Director/Designer: PETER GOOD Illustrator: PETER GOOD Country: USA Description: SPECIAL OLYMPICS WORLD GAMES – SPEZIELLE OLYMPISCHE SPIELE – JEUX OLYMPIQUES SPÉCIAUX

1

2

3

4

5

6

GOLDEN GLOVES

1 CLIENT: DREAMMAKER CUSTOMS DESIGN FIRM: MIRES DESIGN, INC. ART DIRECTOR/DESIGNER: JOSÉ SERRANO ILLUSTRATOR: TRACY SABIN COUNTRY: USA DESCRIPTION: CUSTOM CAR CLUB – CLUB FÜR HANDGEFERTIGTE AUTOS – CLUB DE VOITURES HORS SÉRIE ■ **2** CLIENT: COALITION FOR THE HOMELESS DESIGN FIRM: STUDIO MORRIS ART DIRECTOR: JEFFREY MORRIS DESIGNER: KAORU SATO COUNTRY: USA DESCRIPTION: NON-PROFIT ORGANIZATION – OBDACHLOSENVERBAND – ASSOCIATION POUR LES S.D.F. ■ **3** CLIENT: U.S. ASSOCIATION FOR BLIND ATHLETES DESIGN FIRM/ART DIRECTION/DESIGN: AFTER HOURS CREATIVE COUNTRY: USA DESCRIPTION: U.S. ASSOCIATION OF BLIND ATHLETES – VERBAND DER BLINDEN ATHELETEN – ASSCOCIATION DES ATHLÈTES NON VOYANTS ■ **4** CLIENT: AMERICAN INSTITUTE OF ARCHITECTS DESIGN FIRM: STUDIO FRANCESCA GARCIA-MARQUES ART DIRECTOR/DESIGNER: FRANCESCA GARCIA-MARQUES COUNTRY: USA DESCRIPTION: AMERICAN INSTITUTE OF ARCHITECTS LECTURE SERIES – VORTRAGSREIHE DES AMERIKANI-

7

SCHEN ARCHITEKTEN-INSTITUTS – SÉRIE DE CONFÉRENCES DE L'IINSTITUT AMÉRICAIN DES ARCHITECTS ■ **5** CLIENT: TYPE DIRECTORS CLUB DESIGN FIRM: GERARD HUERTA DESIGN, INC. ART DIRECTORS: ALLAN HALEY, CYNTHIA HOLLANDSWORTH, CAROL WAHLER, MARA KURTZ, SASHA KURTZ, DAVID BERLOW, DIRK ROWNTREE DESIGNER/ILLUSTRATOR: GERARD HUERTA COUNTRY: USA DESCRIPTION: SPECIAL EVENT FOR TYPE DIRECTORS CLUB – SPEZIELLER ANLASS DES TYPE DIRECTORS CLUB – MANIFESTATION SPÉCIALE DU TYPE DIRECTORS CLUB ■ **6** CLIENT: UNITED BROTHERHOOD OF CARPENTERS AND JOINERS DESIGN FIRM: LEVINE AND ASSOC. ART DIRECTOR/DESIGNER: LENA MARKLEY COUNTRY: USA DESCRIPTION: CARPENTERS UNION – ZIMMER-MANNSZUNFT – CONFRÉRIE DES CHARPENTIERS ■ **7** CLIENT: TEXAS PREVENTION PARTNERSHIP DESIGN FIRM: GIBBS BARONET ART DIRECTOR: WILLIE BARONET DESIGNERS: WILLIE BARONET, MICHAEL CONNORS, ALAN WEAVER COUNTRY: USA DESCRIPTION: HEALTH GROUP – GESUNDHEITSWESEN – SANTÉ PUBLIQUE

1 Client: CORUNDUM INTERNATIONAL IDENTITY Design Firm/Art Director/Designer: BYRON JACOBS Country: HONG KONG Industry/Purpose: GEMSTONE TRADING ORGANISATION – EDELSTEIN-HANDELSORGA-NISATION – ORGANISATION POUR LE COMMERCE DES PIERRES PRÉCIEUSES ■ **2** Client: HARTWAY COMPANY Design Firm: SMIT GHORMLEY LOFGREEN DESIGN Art Director/Designer: ART LOFGREEN Country: USA Industry: BICYCLE PARTS MANUFACTURER – HERSTELLER VON FAHRRADTEILEN – FABRICANT DE PIÈCES DÉTACHÉES POUR CYCLES ■ **3** Client: K2 JAPAN Design Firm: MODERN DOG Art Director/Designer: MICHAEL STRASSBURGER Illustrator: MICHAEL STRASSBURGER Country: JAPAN Industry/Purpose: SKI MANUFAC-

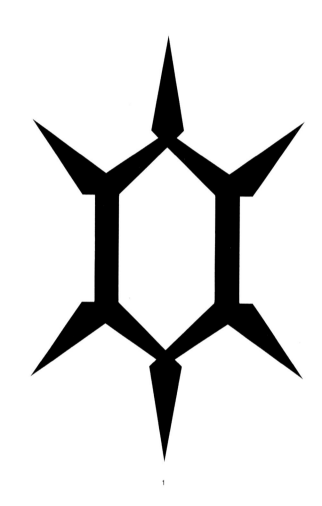

1

TURER – SKI-HERSTELLER – FABRICANT DE SKI ■ **4** Client: BREEZAIR, INC. Design Firm: NAYLOR, DEDONATO & WOLF Art Director/Designer/Illustrator: FRANK PILEGGI Country: USA Industry/Purpose: EVAPORATIVE COOLER MANUFACTURER – HERSTELLER VON LUFTKÜHLGERÄTEN – FABRICANT DE REFRAI-CHISSEURS À AIR. ■ **5** Client: SCIENTIFIC ATLANTA Design Firm: CLEMENT MOK DESIGNS Art Director: MARK CRUMPACKER Designers: SAMANTHA FUETSCH, JOSH DISTLER Project Manager: KAREN ROEHL-SIVAK Country: USA Industry: HARDWARE MANUFACTURER FOR INTERACTIVE TELEVISION – HARDWARE-HERSTEL-LER FÜR INTERAKTIVES FERNSEHEN – FABRICANT DE MATÉRIEL DESTINÉ ÀLA TÉLÉVISION INTERACTIVE

2

3

4

5

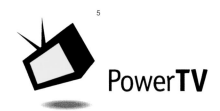

1 Client: SABRE POWERTOOLS Designer: CHAD BAILEY Country: USA Industry: POWER TOOL MANUFACTURER – HERSTELLER VON INDUSTRIEWERKZEUGEN – FABRICANT D'OUTILLAGE INDUSTRIEL. ■ **2** Client: CUSTOM GEAR AND MACHINE Design Firm: THE LARSON GROUP Art Directors: SCOTT DVORAK, KEITH CHRISTIANSON Designer: SCOTT DVORAK Country: USA Industry: GEAR AND MACHINE MANUFACTURE – GETRIEBE- UND MASCHINENHERSTELLUNG – FABRICANT D'ÉQUIPEMENTS ET DE MACHINES ■ **3** Client: PACIFIC COAST FEATHER COMPANY Design Firm: HORNALL ANDERSON DESIGN WORKS, INC. Art Director: JACK ANDERSON Designers: JACK ANDERSON, JULIE LOCK, HEIDI FAVOUR, LEO RAYMUNDO Illustrator: CAROLYN VIBBERT Country: USA Industry: MANUFACURER OF FEATHER DOWN PILLOW AND COMFORTERS – HERSTELLER VON DAUNENBETTEN – FABRICANTS DE DOUVETS ■ **4** Client: WORD ORIGIN, INC. Design Firm: THE DESIGN OFFICE OF WONG & YEO Art Director: VALERIE WONG Designers: VALERIE WONG, CARY CHIAO, KELLY LOW Country: USA Industry: PRODUCER OF HIGH QUALITY GAMES – PRODUZENT ANSPRUCHSVOLLER SPIELE – FABRICANT DE JEUX HAUT DE GAMME ■ **5** Client: PIECES OF EIGHT LIMITED Art Director/Designer: BRET DE THIER Country: NEW ZEALAND Industry: RACING SKIFF MANUFACTURER – HERSTELLER VON SKIFFS – FABRICANT DE SKIFFS ■ **6** Client: NAUTRAK Design Firm: PRINCIPIA GRAPHICA Art Directors: ROBIN RICKABAUGH, HEIDI RICKABAUGH Designers: ROBIN RICKABAUGH, JON OLSEN Country: USA Industry: NAVIGATION EQUIPMENT – NAVIATIONSGERÄTE – EQUIPEMENTS DE NAVIGATION ■ **7** Client: INTEL Design Firm: SMIT GHORMLEY LOFGREEN DESIGN Art Director/Designer: ART LOFGREEN Country: USA Industry: ELECTRONICS MANUFACTURER – HERSTELLER ELEKTRONISCHER GERÄTE – FABRICANT D'APPAREILS ÉLECTRONIQUE ■ **8** Client: ROBERN INC. Design Firm: POLITE DESIGN Designer:

1

KERRY POLITE Country: USA Industry: BATH CABINET MANUFACTURER – HERSTELLER SANITÄRER ANLAGEN – FABRICANT D'INSTALLATIONS SANITAIRES ■ **9** Client: ROOIVALK COMBAT HELIOPTER Design Firm: PENTAGRAPH DESIGN CONSULTANCY Art Director: MARK POSNETT Designer:GARY HARWOOD Country: SOUTH AFRICA Industry: AVIATION COMPANY – HERSTELLER VON HUBSCHRAUBERN – FABRICANT D'HÉLI-COPTÉRES ■ **10** Client: THE CHICAGO BICYCLE COMPANY Design Firm: MAXIMUM MARKETING Art Director: ED HAN Designer/Illustrator: DEIRDRE BOLAND Country: USA Industry: BICYCLE MANUFACTURER – FAHR-RADHERSTELLER – FABRICANT DE CYCLES ■ **11** Client: DPS DIGITAL PREPRESS SERVICES Design Firm: DOGSTAR DESIGN Designer/Illustrator: RODNEY DAVIDSON Country: USA Industry: DIGITAL PRODUCTION SERVICES – DIGITALE PRODUKTIONEN – PRODUCTIONS DIGITALES ■ **12** Client: ROSE CITY PAPER BOX Design Firm: ROOD MORT DESIGN Art Directors/Designers: DON ROOD, PAUL MORT Illustrator: PAUL MORT Country: USA Industry: PAPER BOX MANUFACTURING AND PACKAGING ■ **13** Client: ONKYO CORPORATION Design Firm: HORNALL ANDERSON DESIGN WORKS, INC. Art Director: JACK ANDERSON Designers: JACK ANDERSON, LISA CERVENY, DAVID BATES Country: USA Industry: ELECTRONIC EQUIPMENT MANUFACTURER – HERSTELLER ELEKTRONISCHER GERÄTE – FABRICANT D'APPAREILS ÉLECTRONIQUES ■ **14** Client: FUNK BICYCLES Designer: CHAD BAILEY Country: USA Industry: MOUNTAIN BIKE MANUFACTURER – HERSTELLER VON MOUNTAIN BIKES – FABRICANT DE V.T.T. ■ **15** Client: SNOWBOARDS MANUFACURING COMPANY Design Firm: WTR GRAPHICS Art Director/Designer: FILIP KRIVSKY Country: CZECH REPUBLIC Industry: SNOW-BOARD MANUFACTURER – SNOWBOARD-HERSTELLER – FABRICANT DE SNOWBOARDS ■ **16** Client: RUDOLF NEU GMBH Design Firm: GMS-WERBEAGENTUR Art Director: NORBERT GANZ Designer/Illustrator: CHRISTIAN KREISS Country: GERMANY Industry: LUGGAGE LINE – REISEGEPÄCKSERIE – LIGNE DE BAGAGES

2

3

4

5

6

7

8

9

10

11

12

13

14

15

16

1

2

3

4

5

1 Client: K2 SNOWBOARDS & WAKEBOARDS Design Firm: MODERN DOG Art Directors: BRENT TURNER, MICHAEL STRASSBURGER Designer: MICHAEL STRASSBURGER Country: USA Industry: MANUFACTURER OF SNOWBOARDS AND WAKEBOARDS – HERSTELLER VON SNOWBOARDS UND WAKEBOARDS – FABRICANT DE SNOWBOARDS ET WAKEBOARDS ■ 2 Client: K2 JAPAN Design Firm: MODERN DOG Art Director/Designer: MICHAEL STRASSBURGER Country: JAPAN Industry: MANUFACTURER OF "EXTREME" SKIS – HERSTELLER VON SPEZIAL-SKIS – FABRICANT DE SKI ■ 3 Client: K2 SNOWBOARDS Design Firm: MODERN DOG Art Director/Designer/Illustrator: GEORGE ESTRADA Country: USA Industry: SNOWBOARD MANUFACTURERS –

6

SNOWBOARD HERSTELLER – FABRICANT DE SNOWBOARDS ■ 4 Client: K2 JAPAN Design Firm: MODERN DOG Art Director/Designer/Illustrator: VITTORIO COSTARELLA Country: JAPAN Industry: SKIS AND T-SHIRTS – SKIS UND T-SHIRTS – SKIS ET T-SHIRTS ■ 5 Client: K2 SNOWBOARDS Design Firm: MODERN DOG Art Director: VITTORIO COSTARELLA Designer/Illustrator: VITTORIO COSTARELLA Country: USA Industry: SNOWBOARD MANUFACTURERS – SNOWBOARD HERSTELLER – FABRICANT DE SNOWBOARDS ■ 6 Client: TUNA FISH SIIZ SURFBOARDS Design Firm: HUGHES ADVERTISING INC. Creative Director: RUDY FERNANDEZ Designer: TROY KING Illustrator: TROY KING Country: USA Industry: SURFBOARDS – FABRICANT DE SURFS

1 Client: MEDCHEM Design Firm/Art Direction/Designer/Illustratior: POINT ZERO Country: USA Industry: MEDICAL DEVICE COMPANY – HERSTELLER MEDIZINISCHER GERÄTE – FABRICANT D'ÉQUIPEMENTS MÉDICAUX ■ **2, 6** Client: DELEO CLAY TILE CO. Design Firm: MIRES DESIGN, INC. Art Director/Designer: JOSÉ SERRANO Illustrator: TRACY SABIN Country: USA Industry: PREMIUM CLAY ROOFING TILE MANUFACTURER – HERSTELLER VON DACHZIEGELN UND FLIESEN – FABRICANT DE TUILES ■ **3** Client: BAUER SKATES Design Firm: PINKHAUS DESIGN CORP. Art Director/Designer/Illustrator: JOHN NORMAN Country: USA Industry: ICE

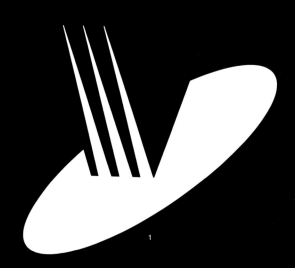

1

SKATE/ROLLERBLADE MANUFACTURER – HERSTELLER VON SCHLITTSCHUHEN UND ROLLERBLADES – FABRICANT DE PATINS À GLACE ET DE PATIN À ROULETTES ■ **4** Client: MIMI WORLD CO., LTD. Design Firm: DOOKIM DESIGN Art Director: DOO H. KIM Designers: DONGIL LEE, SEUNGHEE LEE Country: KOREA Industry: CHILDREN'S TOY MANUFACTURER – HERSTELLER VON KINDERSPIELZEUG – FABRICANT DE JOUETS ■ **5** Client: REED EXHIBITION Design Firm: BUTTON DESIGN COMPANY Art Director/Designer: DOMINIC CARROLL Country: GREAT BRITAIN Industry: PRINTER'S FAIR – MESSE FÜR DAS DRUCKGEWERBE – SALON DE L'IMPRIMERIE

2

3

4

5

6

1 CLIENT: MATT'S HATS DESIGN FIRM: DUFFY DESIGN ART DIRECTOR/DESIGNER/ILLUSTRATOR: NEIL POWELL COUNTRY: USA INDUSTRY: RETAIL APPAREL – HUTLADEN – MODISTE ■ 2 CLIENT: VERDI DESIGN FIRM: RBMM/THE RICHARDS GROUP ART DIRECTOR/DESIGNER/ILLUSTRATOR: LUIS ACEVEDO COUNTRY: MEXICO INDUSTRY: GARDEN FURNITURE – GARTENMÖBEL – MEUBLES DE JARDIN ■ 3 CLIENT: OFFSHORE CONCEPTS DESIGN FIRM: BASLER DESIGN GROUP ART DIRECTOR: BILL BASLER DESIGNERS: BILL BASLER, COLLEEN WENDLING COUNTRY: USA INDUSTRY: HIGH PERFORMANCE BOAT MANUFACTURER – BOOTHERSTELLER – FABRICANT D'OFFSHORES ■ 4 CLIENT: PARADICE DESIGN FIRM: DUFFY DESIGN ART DIRECTOR/DESIGNER/ILLUSTRATOR: KOBE COUNTRY: USA INDUSTRY: RETAIL ICE COMPANY – SPEISEEIS-VERKAUF – VENTES DE GLACES ■ 5 CLIENT: VOIT SPORTS INC. DESIGN FIRM: MIRES DESIGN, INC. ART DIRECTOR: JOSÉ SERRANO DESIGNERS: MIKE BROWER, JOSÉ SERRANO

1

2

3

ILLUSTRATOR: TRACY SABIN COUNTRY: USA INDUSTRY: SPORTING GOODS MANUFACTURER – SPORTARTIKEL-HERSTELLER – FABRICANT D'ARTICLES DE SPORT ■ 6 CLIENT: AVOCET DESIGN FIRM: FROGDESIGN INC. ART DIRECTOR/DESIGNER: MATTHEW CLARK COUNTRY: USA INDUSTRY: MANUFACTURER OF BICYCLE PRODUCTS ■ 7 CLIENT: CRANFORD STREET DESIGN FIRM: MIRES DESIGN, INC. ART DIRECTOR: JOSÉ SERRANO ILLUSTRATOR: TRACY SABIN COUNTRY: USA INDUSTRY: MANUFACTURER OF GAMES AND HOUSEHOLD ITEMS – HERSTELLER VON SPIELEN UND HAUSHALTSGEGENSTÄNDEN – FABRICANT DE JEUX ET D'APPAREILS MÉNAGERS ■ 8 CLIENT: DUKE DESIGN'S DESIGN FIRM: DUFFY DESIGN ART DIRECTOR: NEIL POWELL DESIGNER/ILLUSTRATOR: MISSY WILSON COUNTRY: USA INDUSTRY: SOCK COMPANY – STRUMPFHERSTELLER – FABRICANT DE CHAUSSETTES ■ 9 CLIENT: CONVERSE/TRADE GLOBE SPORTS DESIGN FIRM: SWIETER DESIGN UNITED STATES ART DIRECTOR: JOHN SWIETER DESIGNER: KEVIN FLATT COUNTRY: USA INDUSTRY: SPORTING GOODS – SPORTARTIKEL – ARTICLES DE SPORT

4

5

6

7

8

9

MULTIMEDIA

1

2

3

4

5

1 Client: TIME WARNER INTERACTIVE Design Firm: THE MEDNICK GROUP Art Director: SCOTT MEDNICK Designers: SCOTT MEDNICK, RANDY MOMII, STEVE CURRY Illustrator: RANDY MOMII Photographer: MARK KANE Country: USA Description: COMMUNICATIONS CONGLOMERATE – KOMMUNIKATIONS-KONGLOMERAT – CONGLOMÉRAT SPÉCIALISÉ DANS LES TÉLÉCOMMUNICATIONS ■ 2 Client: CEH Design Firm: LOGVIN DESIGN Art Director/Designer: ANDREY LOGVIN Country: RUSSIA Description: CINEMA AND VIDEO PRODUCTIONS – FILM- UND VIDÉO-PRODUKTIONEN – PRODUCTION DE FILMS ET DE VIDÉOS ■ 3 Client: SEGA Design Firm: THE MEDNICK GROUP Art Director: SCOTT MEDNICK Designer: SCOTT MEDNICK, KEN LOH Illustrator: ELECTRIC PAINT Country: USA Description: COMMUNICATIONS CONGLOMERATE – KOMMUNIKATIONS-KONGLOMERAT –

6

7

8

CONGLOMÉRAT SPÉCIALISÉ DANS LES TÉLÉCOMMUNICATIONS ■ 4 Client: HIT-TV Design Firm: LINIA GRAFIC Art Director/Designer/Illustrator: DMITRY DOLGOV Country: RUSSIA Description: POST-PRODUCTION COMPANY – FILMSCHNITT – SOCIÉTÉ DE POSTPRODUCTION ■ 5 Client: ROCKET SCIENCE Design Firm: THE MEDNICK GROUP Art Director: SCOTT MEDNICK Designers: SCOTT MEDNICK, RANDY MOMII Illustrator: RANDY MOMII Country: USA Description: ROCKET SCIENCE – RAKETENFORSCHUNG – RECHERCHE SUR LES FUSÉES ■ 6–8 Client: METAPHOR PTY LTD Design Firm: GRANT JORGENSEN GRAPHIC DESIGN Art Director/Designer/Illustrator: GRANT JORGENSEN Country: AUSTRALIA Description: MULTIMEDIA FOR CD ROM PRESENTATION – MULTIMEDIA-PRODUKTION FÜR CD ROM – PRODUCTION MULTIMÉDIA POUR CD-ROM

1

2

3

4

5

1 Client: SAN FRANCISCO MUSEUM OF MODERN ART Design Firm: CRONAN DESIGN, INC. Art Director/Illustrator: MICHAEL CRONAN Designers: MICHAEL CRONAN, SUSAN TSUCHIYA, ANTHONY YELL Country: USA Description: MUSEUM – MUSÉE D'ART MODERNE ■ **2** Client: LINNAGALERII Designer: JURI KASS Country: ESTONIA Description: GALLERY – GALERIE ■ **3** Client: SEA SCIENCE CENTER Design Firm: DOGSTAR DESIGN Creative Director: GEORGE FULLER Designer/Illustrator: RODNEY DAVIDSON Country:

6

USA Description: AQUATIC MUSEUM – MUSEUM FÜR MEERESBIOLOGIE – MUSÉE D'OCÉANOGRAPHIE ■ **4** Client: SCHOOL GALLERY Design Firm: LOGVIN DESIGN Art Director/Designer: ANDREY LOGVIN Country: RUSSIA Description: ART PHOTO GALLERY – PHOTOGALERIE – GALERIE DE PHOTOGRAPHIE D'ART ■ **5** Client: AFRICAN AMERICAN MUSEUM Design Firm: RBMM/THE RICHARDS GROUP Designer: LUIS ACEVEDO Country: USA Description: MUSEUM – MUSÉE ■ **6** Client: TOTTORI PREFECTURE Design Firm: KEIZO MATSUI & ASSOC. Art Director: KEIZO MATSUI Designer: GERMAN MONTALVO Country: JAPAN Description: MUSEUM – MUSÉE

1 CLIENT: KIRK ALFORD DESIGN FIRM: DOGSTAR DESIGN DESIGNER/ILLUSTRATOR: RODNEY DAVIDSON COUNTRY: USA BUSINESS: PIANO TECHNICIAN – KLAVIERSTIMMER – ACCORDEUR DE PIANOS ■ **2** CLIENT: KKHG RADIO DESIGN FIRM: SANDSTROM DESIGN ART DIRECTOR: STEVEN SANDSTROM DESIGNER: JENNIFER LYON ILLUSTRATORS: GEORGE CHENEY, JANÉE WARREN COUNTRY: USA DESCRIPTION: CLASSIC ROCK RADIO STATION – RADIOSENDER FÜR KLASSISCHE ROCK-MUSIK – STATION DE RADIO DE ROCK ■ **3** CLIENT: WINDHAM HILL RECORDS DESIGN FIRM: CRONAN DESIGN, INC. ART DIRECTOR: MICHAEL CRONAN ILLUSTRATOR: MICHAEL CRONAN DESIGNERS: MICHAEL CRONAN, BRAD BERBERICH, CINTHIA WEN COUNTRY: USA BUSINESS: RECORD

1

COMPANY – PLATTENFIRMA – MAISON DE DISQUES ■ **4** CLIENT: LEVYPISTE OY DESIGN FIRM: METSÄRANTA ART & DESIGN ART DIRECTOR: ANTTI METSÄRANTA DESIGNER: ANTTI METSÄRANTA COUNTRY: FINLAND BUSINESS: RECORD CONSULTING AND SUPPLYING FOR DEPARTMENT STORES AND SERVICE STATIONS – BERATUNG UND LIEFERUNG VON SCHALLPLATTEN FÜR KAUFHÄUSER UND TANKSTELLENKIOSKE – CONSEIL ET DISTRIBUTION DE DISQUES DANS LES GRANDS MAGASINS ET DES STATIONS-SERVICE. ■ **5** CLIENT: OUR PRICE MUSIC DESIGN FIRM: CDT DESIGN ART DIRECTOR: NICHOLAS THIRKELL DESIGNERS: NICHOLAS THIRKELL, NEIL WALKER, IAIN CROCKART COUNTRY: GREAT BRITAIN BUSINESS: MUSIC RETAILER – MUSIKLADEN – MAGASIN DE MUSIQUE

2

3

4

5

1 CLIENT: MUSICAL-COMPANY ART DIRECTOR/DESIGNER: GÜNTER JACKI COUNTRY: GERMANY DESCRIPTION: CONCERT AGENCY – KONZERTAGENTUR – AGENCE DE CONCERTS ■ **2** CLIENT: MICHAEL BOB DESIGN FIRM: *)MEDIAWERK ART DIRECTOR: LUCAS BUCHHOLZ DESIGNER: ZACHARIAS COUNTRY: GERMANY DESCRIPTION: MUSIC CLUB – MUSIK-CLUB – CLUB DE MUSIQUE ■ **3** CLIENT: DEWIN TIBBS DESIGN FIRM: DOGSTAR DESIGN DESIGNER/ILLUSTRATOR: RODNEY DAVIDSON COUNTRY: USA DESCRIPTION: OPERATIC BARITONE – OPERNSÄNGER – CHANTEUR D'OPÉRA ■ **4** CLIENT: PAN TRINBAGO DESIGN FIRM/ART DIRECTOR/DESIGNER/ILLUSTRATOR: RUSSEL HALFHIDE COUNTRY: TRINIDAD TOBAGO DESCRIPTION: MUSICAL ORGANIZATION – MUSIK-VERBAND – SOCIÉTÉ DE MUSIQUE ■ **5** DESIGNER: LAURA A. STURZL COUNTRY: USA INDUSTRY/PURPOSE (STUDENT PROJECT): RECORD COMPANY, RECORDING STUDIO – SCHALLPLATTENFIRMA, AUFNAHMESTUDIO – STUDIO D'ENREGISTREMENT, MAISON DE DISQUES ■ **6** CLIENT: Y-NOS RECORDS DESIGN FIRM: FARNET HART DESIGN, INC. ART DIRECTOR: WINNIE HART ILLUSTRATOR: T.J. TODD COUNTRY: USA DESCRIPTION: RECORD COMPANY – SCHALLPLATTENFIRMA – MAISON DE DISQUES ■ **7** CLIENT: DALLAS SYMPHONY ORCHESTRA DESIGN FIRM: RBMM/THE RICHARDS GROUP ART DIRECTOR/DESIGNER: HORACIO COBOS COUNTRY: USA DESCRIPTION: ORCHESTRA – ORCHESTER – ORCHESTRE ■ **8** CLIENT: EASTWEST RECORDS DESIGN FIRM: FACTOR DESIGN ART DIRECTOR/DESIGNER: RÜDIGER GÖTZ ILLUSTRATOR: RÜDIGER GÖTZ COUNTRY: GERMANY DESCRIPTION: POPSINGER – POPINTERPRET – CHAN-

1

TEUR POP ■ **9** CLIENT: THE TAB TWO DESIGN FIRM: BÜRO FÜR ALLES KREATIVE & VERRÜCKTE DESIGNER: JAN WILKER COUNTRY: GERMANY DESCRIPTION: MUSICAL GROUP – MUSIKGRUPPE – GROUPE DE MUSIQUE ■ **10** CLIENT: GOD'S FAVORITE DOG ART DIRECTORS/DESIGNERS: MARKUS HEINBACH, HANS SURES COUNTRY: GERMANY DESCRIPTION: HIP HOP BAND – GROUPE DE HIP HOP ■ **11** CLIENT: RAINBOW BRIDGE DESIGN FIRM: JOHN EVANS DESIGN ART DIRECTOR/DESIGNER: JOHN EVANS ILLUSTRATOR: JOHN EVANS COUNTRY: USA DESCRIPTION: JAZZ BENEFIT CONCERT – BENEFIZ-JAZZKONZERT – CONCERT DE JAZZ À BUT DE BIENFAI-SANCE ■ **12** CLIENT: JACK MCDOWELL STICK FIGURE DESIGN FIRM: VSA PARTNERS, INC. ART DIRECTORS: JAMES KOVAL, JACK MCDOWELL DESIGNERS: JAMES KOVAL, STEVE RYAN COUNTRY: USA DESCRIPTION: MUSICAL GROUP, "STICK FIGURE" – MUSIKGRUPPE – GROUPE DE MUSIQUE ■ **13** CLIENT: HOTEL PRINCIPE FELIPE DESIGN FIRM: DAVID CARTER DESIGN ART DIRECTOR: LORI B. WILSON, BRIAN MOSS DESIGNER: BRIAN MOSS ILLUSTRATOR: ROBERT PRINCE COUNTRY: SPAIN DESCRIPTION: JAZZ BAR ■ **14, 16** CLIENTS: THE MAGIC MUSHROOMS (14), THE SPACEFROGS (16) DESIGN FIRM: *)MEDIAWERK ART DIRECTOR: LUCAS BUCHHOLZ DESIGNER: ZACHARIAS COUNTRY: GERMANY DESCRIPTION: RECORD LABEL – PLATTENLABEL – LABEL DE PRO-DUCTION ■ **15** CLIENT: THE BLUE RIBBON SOUNDWORKS DESIGN FIRM: CREATIVE R+D ART DIRECTOR/DESIGNER: PHIL SCOPP ILLUSTRATOR: PHIL SCOPP COUNTRY: USA DESCRIPTION: COMPUTER SOFTWARE FOR MUSIC PRO-DUCTION – COMPUTER-SOFTWARE FÜR DIE PRODUKTION VON MUSIK – LOGICIEL DE PRODUCTION MUSICALE

2

3

4

NICKTONE MUSIC, LTD.

5

Y-NOS

6

7

8

9

10

11

12

spike's
JAZZ BAR

13

14

15

16

1 CLIENT: FRENCH PAPER DESIGN FIRM: CHARLES S. ANDERSON DESIGN COMPANY ART DIRECTOR: CHARLES S. ANDERSON DESIGNERS: CHARLES S. ANDERSON, JOEL TEMPLIN COUNTRY: USA INDUSTRY: PAPER MANUFACTURER – PAPIERHERSTELLER – FABRICANT DE PAPIER ■ 2 CLIENT: WEYERHAEUSER FINE PAPER DESIGN FIRM: NAYLOR, DEDONATO & WOLF ART DIRECTOR/DESIGNER: BILL HEALEY ILLUSTRATOR: JOHN THOMPSON COUNTRY: USA INDUSTRY: PAPER MANUFACTURER – PAPIERHERSTELLER – FABRICANT DE PAPIER ■ 3 CLIENT: STRATH-MORE PAPER COMPANY DESIGN FIRM: MICHAEL SCHWAB DESIGN ART DIRECTOR: SARAH KLOMAN DESIGNER/ILLUSTRATOR: MICHAEL SCHWAB DESIGN AGENCY: DESIGNFRAME COUNTRY: USA INDUSTRY: PAPER MANUFACTURER – PAPIERHERSTELLER – FABRICANT DE PAPIER ■ 4 CLIENT: MEAD COATED PAPERS DESIGN FIRM: VSA

1

PARTNERS ART DIRECTOR: DANA ARNETT DESIGNERS: CURT SCHREIBER, KEN FOX COUNTRY: USA INDUSTRY: PAPER MANUFACTURER – PAPIERHERSTELLER – FABRICANT DE PAPIER ■ 5 CLIENT: PAPIERMÜHLE GMUND DESIGN FIRM: FACTOR DESIGN ART DIRECTORS/DESIGNERS: RÜDIGER GÖTZ, OLAF STEIN ILLUSTRATOR: RÜDIGER GÖTZ COUNTRY: GERMANY INDUSTRY: PAPER MANUFACTURER – PAPIERHERSTELLER – FABRICANT DE PAPIER ■ 6 CLIENT: FOUND STUFF PAPERWORKS DESIGN FIRM: MIRES DESIGN, INC. ART DIRECTOR/DESIGNER: JOSÉ SERRANO ILLUSTRATOR: TRACY SABIN COUNTRY: USA INDUSTRY: HANDMADE, RECYCLED PAPER PRODUCTS – HANDGEMACHTE PRODUKTE AUS WIEDERVERWERTETEM PAPIER – PRODUITS FAITS MAIN EN PAPIER RECY-CLÉ ■ 7 CLIENT: WATSON PAPER DESIGN FIRM: VAUGHN WEDEEN CREATIVE ART DIRECTOR/DESIGNER/ILLUSTRATOR: RICK VAUGHN COUNTRY: USA INDUSTRY: PAPER MANUFACTURER – PAPIERHERSTELLER – FABRICANT DE PAPIER

2

3

MGENERATIONSD

4

5

6

7

1

2

3

1 Client: SCOTT GATZKE PHOTOGRAPHY Design Firm: ZAUHAR DESIGN Art Director/Designer/Illustrator: DAVID ZAUHAR Country: USA Business: PHOTOGRAPHY STUDIO – PHOTO-ATELIER – STUDIO DE PHOTOGRA- PHIE ■ 2 Client: OLAF FIPPINGER Design Firm: FACTOR DESIGN Art Director: RÜDIGER GÖTZ Designer: RÜDIGER GÖTZ Illustrator: RÜDIGER GÖTZ Country: GERMANY Business: FREELANCE PHOTO DESIGNER – FREIER PHOTODESIGNER – PHOTOGRAPHE INDÉPENDANT ■ 3 Client: ERIC PEARLE PHOTOGRAPHER Design Firm: GIBBS BARONET Art Director: WILLIE BARONET Designer: META NEWHOUSE Country: USA Business: PROFESSIONAL SERVICE PHOTOGRAPHER – PROFI-PHOTOGRAPH – PHOTOGRAPHE PROFESSIONNEL

1 Client: J.W. Fry Design Firm: PINKHAUS DESIGN CORP. Art Director/Designer: JOHN NORMAN Country: USA Description: PHOTOGRAPHER – PHOTOGRAPH – PHOTOGRAPHE ■ 2 Client: RABBIT PHOTO Design Firm: CLEMENT MOK DESIGN Senior Designer: ANDREW CAWRSE Country: USA Description: PHOTOGRAPHER – PHOTOGRAPH – PHOTOGRAPHE ■ 3 Client: SCHOENFELD PHOTOGRAPHY Design Firm: ARROWOOD DESIGN Art Director/Designer: SCOTT ARROWOOD Country: USA Description: PHOTOGRAPHER – PHOTOGRAPH – PHOTOGRAPHE ■ 4 Client: ROBIN HOOD Design Firm: ROBERTSON DESIGN Art Directors: JOHN ROBERTSON, JEFF CARROLL Designer: JEFF CARROLL Country: USA Description: PHOTOGRAPHER – PHOTOGRAPH – PHOTOGRAPHE ■ 5 Client: ADVERTISING PHOTOGRAPHERS OF AMERICA Design Firm: BLACKDOG Art Director/Designer: MARK FOX Country: USA Description: PHOTOGRAPHERS' ASSOCIATION – VERBAND DER AMERIKANISCHEN WERBEPHOTOGRAPHEN – ASSOCIATION DES PHOTOGRAPHES AMÉRICAINS DE PUBLICITÉ ■ 6 Client: R AND R IMAGES Design Firm: SMIT GHORMLEY LOFGREEN DESIGN Art Director/Designer: ART LOFGREEN Country: USA Description: PHOTOGRAPHER – PHOTOGRAPH – PHOTOGRAPHE ■ 7 Client: DETLEF ODENHAUSEN

1

PHOTOGRAPHIE Design Firm: DESIGN AHEAD Designer: RALF STUMPF Country: GERMANY Description: PHOTOGRAPHER – PHOTOGRAPH – PHOTOGRAPHE ■ 8 Client: TOP DOGS PRODUCTIONS Design Firm: RBMM/THE RICHARDS GROUP Designer: PAMELA CHANG Country: USA Description: PHOTOGRAPHER'S STUDIO – PHOTOATELIER – STUDIO DE PHOTOGRAPHIE ■ 9 Client: JEFF OTT PHOTOGRAPHY Design Firm: DENNARD CREATIVE Art Director: BOB DENNARD Designer: CHRIS WOOD Country: USA Description: PHOTOGRAPHER – PHOTOGRAPH – PHOTOGRAPHE ■ 10 Client: RICHARD REENS Design Firm: RBMM/THE RICHARD GROUP Art Director/Designer/Illustrator: LUIS ACEVEDO Country: USA Description: PHOTOGRAPHER – PHOTOGRAPH – PHOTOGRAPHE ■ 11 Client: TIM DOTY Design Firm: NANCY STENTZ DESIGN Art Director/Designer/Illustrator: NANCY STENTZ Country: USA Description: PHOTOGRAPHER – PHOTOGRAPH – PHOTOGRAPHE ■ 12 Client: EPSTEIN PHOTOGRAPHY Design Firm: POLLARD DESIGN Art Director/Designer: JEFF POLLARD Country: USA Description: PHOTOGRAPHY STUDIO – PHOTO-ATELIER – STUDIO DE PHOTOGRAPHIE ■ 13 Client: RALPH DANIEL PHOTOGRAPHY Design Firm: DEEP DESIGN Art Directors: RICK GRIMSLEY, MARK STEINGRUBER Designer: RICK GRIMSLEY Country: USA Description: PHOTOGRAPHER – PHOTOGRAPH – PHOTOGRAPHE

2

schoenfeld

3

4

5

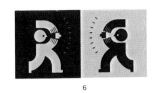

6

7

8

PHOTTOGRAPHY

9

10

11

12

13

1

2

3

4

5

1 Client: CHATHAM PRINTING Design Firm: PETER GOOD GRAPHIC DESIGN Art Director: PETER GOOD Designers: JANET CUMMINGS GOOD, CHRISTOPHER HYDE Country: USA Industry: PRINTER – DRUCKEREI – IMPRIMERIE ■ **2** Client: BORDEAUX PRINTERS Design Firm: MIRES DESIGN, INC. Art Director/Designer: JOSE SERRANO Country: USA Industry: PRINTER – DRUCKEREI – IMPRIMERIE ■ **3** Client: COLORMARK Design Firm: DANNY KAMERATH DESIGN Art Director/Designer/Illustrator: DANNY KAMERATH Country: USA Industry: PRINTER – DRUCKEREI – IMPRIMERIE ■ **4** Client: CRITICAL IMPRESSIONS Design Firm: ROBERTSON DESIGN Art Directors: JEFF CARROLL, JOHN ROBERTSON Designer: JEFF CARROLL Country: USA Industry: PRINTER – DRUCKEREI – IMPRIMERIE ■ **5** Client: RIGHT READING PREPRESS Design Firm: KILMER, KILMER & JAMES, INC. Designer: RICHARD KILMER Country: USA Industry: DIGITAL PREPRESS AND PRODUCTION SERVICE – DIGITALE HERSTELLUNG VON DRUCKVORLAGEN – PRODUCTION DIGITALE DE MAQUETTES ■ **6** Client: SOUTH PRESS Design Firm: PETERSON & COMPANY Art Director/Designer: JAN

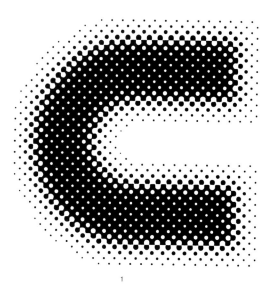

1

WILSON Country: USA Industry: PRINTER – DRUCKEREI – IMPRIMERIE ■ **7** Client: STIL MATBAACILIK A.S. Design Firm: VALÖR TASARIM LTD. STI. Art Director/Designer: SAVAS CEKIC Country: TURKEY Industry: PRINTER – DRUCKEREI – IMPRIMERIE ■ **8** Client: ENGRAVED STATIONERY MANUFACTURERS ASSOCIATION Design Firm: POLLARD DESIGN Art Director: JEFF POLLARD Designer: JEFF POLLARD Country: USA Industry: MANUFACTURERS ASSOCIATION – VERBAND VON SCHREIBWARENHERSTELLERN – ASSOCIATION DES PAPETIERS ■ **9** Client: PRINTECH Design Firm: VERONICA D'OREY COMUNICAÇÃO VISUAL Art Director: VERONICA KUMLIN D'OREY Designer: VERONICA KUMLIN D'OREY Country: BRASIL Industry: SECURITY PRINTER OF CHECK BOOKS, BAR CODES – DRUCKEREI FÜR FÄLSCHUNGSSICHERE DOKUMENTE – IMPRESSION DE CARNETS DE CHÈQUES ■ **10** Client: GROSSBERG TYLER LITHOGRAPHERS Design Firm: CONCEPTUAL REALITY Art Director/Designer: JANI DREWFS Illustrator: BRIAN O'NEILL Country: USA Industry: PRINTERS, LITHOGRAPHERS – DRUCKEREI UND LITHOANSTALT – IMPRIMEURS-LITHOGRAPHES

2

3

4

5

6

7

8

PRINTECH

9

GROSSBERG TYLER

LITHOGRAPHERS

10

1

2

3

4

5

6

7

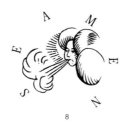

8

9

10

11

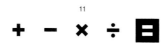

12

1 CLIENT: BREDBERG AUTO WERKS DESIGN FIRM/ART DIRECTOR/DESIGNER: BRIAN LANE COUNTRY: USA DESCRIPTION: AUTO MECHANIC – AUTOMECHANIKER – MÉCANICIEN ■ 2 CLIENT: FUTURE 1 DESIGN FIRM: MACVICAR DESIGN AND COMMUNICATIONS ART DIRECTOR: JOHN VANCE DESIGNER: JOHN VANCE ILLUSTRATOR: JOHN VANCE COUNTRY: USA DESCRIPTION: INSURANCE COMPANY, INSURANCE AGENTS – VERSICHERUNGS-GESELLSCHAFT, VERSICHERUNGSAGENTEN – AGENTS D'ASSURANCE ■ 3 CLIENT: TECHNISCHE ROHRREINI-GUNG GMBH DESIGNER: BETTINA NEUSTADT COUNTRY: GERMANY DESCRIPTION: WATER PIPE CLEANING COMPANY – ROHRREINIGUNG – ENTREPRISE DE NETTOYAGE DE TUYAUX ■ 4 CLIENT: GO SPOT GO CAR WASH DESIGN FIRM: SANDSTROM DESIGN ART DIRECTOR/DESIGNER: STEVEN SANDSTROM COUNTRY: USA DESCRIPTION: SELF-SERVE AND DRIVE-THROUGH CAR WASH – AUTOWASCHANLAGE MIT SELBSTBEDIENUNG – STATION DE LAVAGE SELF-SERVICE ■ 5 CLIENT: DATAQUICK DESIGN FIRM: LAURA COE DESIGN ASSOCIATES ART DIRECTOR: TRACY CASTLE DESIGNER/ILLUSTRATOR: RYOICHI YOTSUMOTO COUNTRY: USA DESCRIPTION: INSURANCE AGENTS – VERSICHERUNGSAGENTEN – AGENTS D'ASSURANCE ■ 6 CLIENT: DOWNTOWN IMPORT SERVICE DESIGN FIRM: EAT DESIGN, L.L.C. ART DIRECTOR: PATRICE EILTS-JOBE DESIGNERS: PATRICE EILTS-JOBE, KEVIN TRACY ILLUSTRATOR: KEVIN TRACY COUNTRY: USA DESCRIPTION: IMPORT CAR SERVICE – WERKSTATT FÜR IMPORTAUTOS – STATION-SERVICE POUR VOITURES D'IMPORTATION ■ 7 CLIENT: ILLUMINA, INC. DESIGN FIRM: RBMM/THE RICHARDS GROUP ART DIRECTOR/DESIGNER: HORACIO COBOS COUNTRY: USA DESCRIPTION: LIGHTING COMPANY FOR BUILDING EXTERIORS – HERSTELLER VON AUSSENBELEUCHTUNGEN – FABRICANT D'É-

13

14

CLAIRAGES EXTÉRIEURS ■ 8 CLIENT: SEAMEN SEEBESTATTUNGSINSTITUT DESIGN FIRM: ROBENS, HONRODT. DIE ART AGENTUR. ART DIRECTOR/DESIGNER/ILLUSTRATOR: CHRISTIANE ROBENS COUNTRY: GERMANY DESCRIPTION: FUNERALS ON SEA – SEEBESTATTUNGEN – INSTITUT DE POMPES FUNÈBRES EN HAUTE MER ■ 9 CLIENT: VENTUS SEEBESTATTUNGSINSTITUT DESIGN FIRM: ROBENS, HONRODT. DIE ART AGENTUR. ART DIRECTOR/DESIGNER/ILLUSTRATOR: CHRISTIANE ROBENS COUNTRY: GERMANY DESCRIPTION: FUNERAL HOME – BESTATTUNGSINSTITUT – POMPES FUNÈBRES ■ 10 CLIENT: DATAQUICK DESIGN FIRM: LAURA COE DESIGN ASSOCIATES ART DIRECTOR: TRACY CASTLE DESIGNER/ILLUSTRATOR: RYOICHI YOTSUMOTO COUNTRY: USA DESCRIPTION: INVESTORS – ANLAGEBERATER – CONSEIL EN PLACEMENTS ■ 11 CLIENT: SUM SYSTEMS DESIGN FIRM: SPANGLER ASSOCIATES ART DIRECTOR/DESIGNER/ILLUSTRATOR: MICHAEL CONNORS COUNTRY: USA DESCRIPTION: ACCOUNTING AND MANAGEMENT SYTEMS – BUCHFÜHRUNGS- UND MANAGEMENT-SYSTEME – SYSTÈMES DE COMPTABILITÉ ET DE MANAGEMENT ■ 12 CLIENT: STEVENS SEARCY HILL DESIGN FIRM: GRANT JORGENSEN GRAPHIC DESIGN ART DIRECTOR/DESIGNER: GRANT JORGENSEN COUNTRY: AUSTRALIA DESCRIPTION: ACCOUNTANTS – BUCHFÜHRUNG – CABINET D'EXPERTS-COMPTABLES ■ 13 CLIENT: REALIZE CORPORATION DESIGN FIRM: SHIGEO KATSUOKA DESIGN STUDIO ART DIRECTOR/DESIGNER: SHIGEO KATSUOKA COUNTRY: JAPAN DESCRIPTION: WATER TREATMENT COMPANY – GEWÄSSER-SANIERUNGSUNTERNEHMEN – ENTREPRISE DE TRAITEMENT DES EAUX USÉES ■ 14 CLIENT: THE MEIJI MUTUAL LIFE INSURANCE COMPANY DESIGN FIRM: SHIGEO KATSUOKA DESIGN STUDIO ART DIRECTOR/DESIGNER: SHIGEO KATSUOKA COUNTRY: JAPAN DESCRIPTION: LIFE INSURANCE COMPANY – LEBENSVERSICHERUNGSGESELLSCHAFT – SOCIÉTÉ D'ASSURANCE VIE

1 CLIENT: NEOTURF, INC. DESIGN FIRM: SIBLEY/PETEET, INC. ART DIRECTOR/DESIGNER/ILLUSTRATOR: TOM HOUGH COUNTRY: USA DESCRIPTION: LANDSCAPING SERVICE — LANDSCHAFTSGÄRTNER — JARDINIERS-PAYSAGISTES ■ 2 CLIENT: METROWEST LANDSCAPE COMPANY DESIGN FIRM: SULLIVANPERKINS ART DIRECTOR/DESIGNER: ART GARCIA COUNTRY: USA DESCRIPTION: LANDSCAPE COMPANY — LANDSCHAFTSGÄRTNER — JARDINIERS-PAYSA-GISTES ■ 3 CLIENT: PIERRE CORNUZ DESIGN FIRM: 4D ART DIRECTOR/DESIGNER/ILLUSTRATOR: ERIC FESSLER COUNTRY: SWITZERLAND DESCRIPTION: BOAT REPAIR AND MAINTENANCE — BOOTSWERFT — CHANTIER NAVAL ■

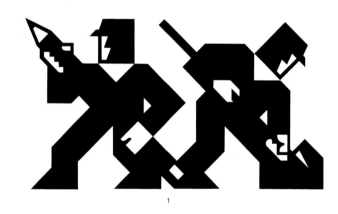

1

4 CLIENT: MONTGOMERY SECURITIES DESIGN FIRM: GOODBY SILVERSTEIN & PARTNERS ART DIRECTORS: PAUL CURTIN, ROD PRICE DESIGNER: PETER LOCKE ILLUSTRATOR: CHRISTOPHER WORMELL COUNTRY: USA DESCRIPTION: SECURITIES — WERTPAPIERE — TITRES ■ 5 CLIENT: PROGRESS ELECTRIC DESIGN FIRM: VSA PARTNERS, INC. ART DIRECTOR: JAMES KOVAL DESIGNERS: JAMES KOVAL, JENNIFER WEISS COUNTRY: USA DESCRIPTION: ELECTRIC CONTRACTOR — ELEKTRIKER — ÉLECTRICIEN ■ 6 CLIENT: MIDLAND RESEARCH DESIGN FIRM: MIRES DESIGN, INC. ART DIRECTOR/DESIGNER: JOSÉ SERRANO ILLUSTRATOR: TRACY SABIN COUNTRY: USA DESCRIPTION: CORPORATE RESEARCH — WIRTSCHAFTSANALYSEN — INSTITUT DE RECHERCHES FINANCIÈRES

2

A/P ENTREPRISE

3

Montgomery
The Other Street

4

5

6

1

2

3

4

5

1 Client: MOUNTAINEERS BOOKS Design Firm: MICHAEL COURTNEY DESIGN Art Director/Designer: MICHAEL COURTNEY Illustrators: MICHAEL COURTNEY, BRIAN O'NEILL Country: USA Description: PUBLISHERS OF OUTDOOR TITLES – VERLAG VON BÜCHERN ÜBER NATUR UND LANDSCHAFT – EDITION DE LIVRES SUR LA NATURE ET LES PAYSAGES ■ **2** Client: KAHOKU SHIMPO PUBLISHING CO. Design Firm: NIPPON DESIGN CENTER, INC. Art Director: KAZUMASA NAGAI Designer: KAZUMASA NAGAI Country: JAPAN Description: PUBLISHERS – VERLAG – MAISON D'ÉDITION ■ **3** Client: HAWK'S NEST PUBLISHING Design Firm: LAMBERT DESIGN STUDIO Art Director: CHRISTIE LAMBERT Designer: JOY CATHEY PRICE Country: USA Description:

6

PUBLISHER OF INTERNAL MATERIALS FOR SCHOOL – SCHULBUCHVERLAG – MAISON D'ÉDITION DE LIVRES SCOLAIRES ■ **4** Client: LEONHARDT & KERN ALPHA GMBH Design Firm: JOERG BAUER DESIGN Art Director: JOERG BAUER Designer: JOERG BAUER Country: GERMANY Description: PUBLISHER – VERLAG – MAISON D'ÉDITION ■ **5** Client: KORSAN YAYINCILIK Design Firm: VALÖR TASARIM LTD. STI. Art Director/Designer: SAVAS CEKIC Country: TURKEY Description: PUBLISHER – VERLAG – MAISON D'ÉDITION ■ **6** Client: COLLEGE OF DESIGN MAGAZINE Design Firm: COLLEGE OF DESIGN, IOWA STATE UNIVERSITY Designers: ANGIE BURR, JASON ENDRES, BRAD JOHNSON, KELLY KONWINSKI, SALLY SLAVENS Country: USA Description: SELF-FUNDED STUDENT PUBLICATION – STUDENTENZEITSCHRIFT – MAGAZINE DES ÉTUDIANTS

1 Client: MOSCOW PREPRESS SERVICES, INC. Design Firm: LINIA GRAFIC Art Director: DMITRY DOLGOV Designer: DMITRY DOLGOV Illustrator: DMITRY DOLGOV Country: RUSSIA Industry: PREPRESS SERVICE COMPANY – HERSTELLUNG VON DRUCKVORLAGEN – PRODUCTION DE MAQUETTES ■ 2 Client: THE WYATT COMPANY Design Firm: MACVICAR DESIGN AND COMMUNICATIONS Art Director/Designer: JOHN VANCE Illustrator: JOHN VANCE Country: USA Industry: HEALTHCARE PUBLISHING – HERAUSGABE VON PUBLIKATIONEN ZUM THEMA GESUNDHEIT – EDITION DE PUBLICATIONS SUR LA SANTÉ ■ 3 Client: READER'S MAGAZINE Design Firm: YE DESIGN Art Director: XIAO YONG Designer: XIAO YONG Country: CHINA Industry: PUBLISHER – VERLAG – MAISON D'ÉDITION ■ 4 Client: EL NUEVO DÍA Art Director: ROBERTO ACEVEDO Illustrator: ROBERTO ACEVEDO Country: PUERTO RICO Industry: NEWSPAPER – ZEITUNG – JOURNAL ■ 5 Client: HARCOURT BRACE & CO. Design Firm: MIRES DESIGN, INC. Art Director: JOSÉ SERRANO Designer: JOSÉ SERRANO Country: USA Industry: PUBLISHERS – VERLAG – MAISON D'ÉDITION ■ 6 Client: BLACK SPARROW PRESS (STUDENT PROJECT) Art Director: GABY BRINK Designer: GABY BRINK Country: USA Industry: BOOK PUBLISHERS – BUCHVERLAG – MAISON D'ÉDITION ■ 7 Client: ARIADNA PUBLISHERS Design Firm/Art Direction/Design: SHTAB GROUP Country: RUSSIA Industry: PUBLISHING

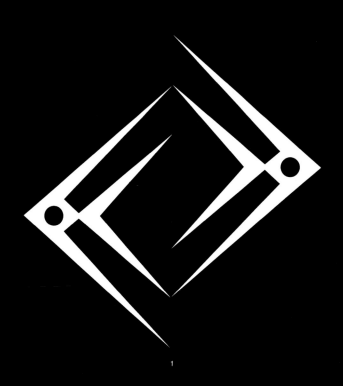

1

COMPANY – VERLAG – MAISON D'ÉDITION ■ 8 Client: LINE MAGAZINE Design Firm: NFQ/2PRINT Art Director: SERGEI KUZHAVSKY Designer: SERGEI KUZHAVSKY Country: RUSSIA Industry: MAGAZINE – ZEITSCHRIFT – MAGAZINE ■ 9 Client: WELLINGTON PUBLISHING Design Firm: RBMM/THE RICHARDS GROUP Art Director/Designer: DICK MITCHELL Country: USA Industry: BOOK PUBLISHERS – VERLAG – MAISON D'ÉDITION ■ 10 Client: MEDIA & EDITORIAL PROJECTS LIMITED Design Firm: RUSSEL HALFHIDE Art Director/Designer/Illustrator: RUSSEL HALFHIDE Country: TRINIDAD TOBAGO Industry: PUBLISHING – VERLAG – MAISON D'ÉDITION ■ 11 Client: TVIORDY ZNAK PUBLISHERS Design Firm: NFQ/2PRINT Art Director/Designer: SERGEI KUZHAVSKY Country: RUSSIA Industry: PUBLISHERS – VERLAG – MAISON D'ÉDI-TION ■ 12 Client: PICTOGRAPHICS Design Firm: CLARKSON CREATIVE Art Director/Designer: LARRY CLARKSON Illustrator: LARRY CLARKSON Country: USA Industry: PUBLISHER OF OUTDOOR IMAGES AND PUBLICATIONS – VERLAG FÜR LANDSCHAFTSBILDER UND -PUBLIKATIONEN – MAISON D'ÉDITION SPÉCIAL-ISÉE DANS LES IMAGES DE PAYSAGES ■ 13 Client: CORPORATION FOR CULTURAL LITERACY Design Firm: JON WELLS ASSOCIATES Art Director/Designer: JON WELLS Illustrator: MICHAEL SCHWAB Country: USA Industry: PUBLISHER OF CHILDREN'S BOOKS – KINDERBUCHVERLAG – EDITION DE LIVRES D'ENFANTS

2

3

4

5

6

7

8

9

10

11

12

13

14

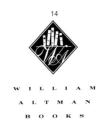

1 Client: HARCOURT BRACE & COMPANY Design Firm: MIRES DESIGN, INC. Art Director: SCOTT MIRES Designers: SCOTT MIRES, JOSÉ SERRANO Illustrator: TRACY SABIN Country: USA Description: TEXTBOOK PUBLISHER – LEHRBUCHVERLAG – MAISON D'ÉDITION DE LIVRES SCOLAIRES ■ **2** Client: NISAN PUBLICATIONS Art Director/Designer: BÜLENT ERKMEN Country: TURKEY Description: PUBLISHER –

1

2

3

VERLAG – MAISON D'ÉDITION ■ **3** Client: AIM – ACHIEVING INSTRUCTIONAL MASTERY Design Firm: ARROWOOD DESIGN Art Director/Designer: SCOTT ARROWOOD Country: USA Description: EDUCATION – BILDUNG – ÉDUCATION ■ **4–6** Client: IMA PRESS Design Firm: KITAJEVA ART-DESIGN STUDIO Art Director/ Designer: JELENA KITAJEVA Illustrator: JELENA KITAJEVA Country: RUSSIA Description: ART-DESIGN GALLERY AND PUBLISHING HOUSE – KUNSTGALERIE UND VERLAG – GALERIE D'ART ET MAISON D'ÉDITION

4

5

6

1

2

3

4

5

6

7

8

9

1 Client: PITCHFORK DEVELOPMENT INC. Design Firm: THE WELLER INSTITUTE FOR THE CURE OF DESIGN Art Directors: DON WELLER, CHIKAKO WELLER Designer/Illustrator: DON WELLER Country: USA Business: CONSTRUCTION AND REAL ESTATE DEVELOPMENT – BAU- UND IMMOBILIENGESELLSCHAFT – BÂTIMENT ET SOCIÉTÉ IMMOBILIÈRE ■ 2 Client: DATAQUICK Design Firm: LAURA COE DESIGN ASSOCIATES Art Director: ROBBIE ATKINS Designer/Illustrator: RYOICHI YOTSUMOTO Country: USA Business: REAL ESTATE, PORT-FOLIO MANAGEMENT – IMMOBILIEN, PORTFOLIO MANAGEMENT – SOCIÉTÉ IMMOBILIÈRE ET GESTION DE TITRES ■ 3 Client: WESTCLIFF CORPORATION LIMITED Design Firm: GRANT JORGENSEN GRAPHIC DESIGN Art Director/Designer: GRANT JORGENSEN Country: AUSTRALIA Business: DEVELOPMENT COMPANY – IMMOBILIENGESELLSCHAFT – SOCIÉTÉ IMMOBILIÈRE ■ 4 Client: JAMES RIVER TOWN CENTER Design Firm: SWIETER DESIGN UNITED STATES Art Director: JOHN SWIETER Designers: MARK FORD, JOHN SWIETER Country: USA Business: SHOPPING CENTER ■ 5 Client: DENRO Design Firm: THINKING CAPS Art Director: ANN MORTON Designer/Illustrator: ANN MORTON Country: USA Business: MASTER PLANNED RESIDENTIAL

10

DEVELOPER – WOHNUNGSBAU-UNTERNEHMUNG – ENTREPRISE DE CONSTRUCTION ■ 6 Client: THE URBAN GROUP Design Firm: DEEP DESIGN Designer: RICK GRIMSLEY Country: USA Business: COMMERCIAL REAL ESTATE DEVELOPER – IMMOBILIENGESELLSCHAFT – SOCIÉTÉ IMMOBILIÈRE ■ 7 Client: ANITA FREY PROPERTY MANAGEMENT Design Firm: GRETEMAN GROUP Art Director: SONIA GRETEMAN, JAMES STRANGE Country: USA Business: PROPERTY MANAGEMENT – IMMOBILIENVERWALTUNG – ADMINISTRATION DE BIEN IMMOBILIERS ■ 8 Client: DAVIDSON COMMUNITIES Design Firm: MIRES DESIGN, INC. Art Director: SCOTT MIRES Designer: CATHERINE SACHS, SCOTT MIRES Illustrator: Country: USA Business: REAL ESTATE DEVELOPMENT – IMMOBILIENGESELLSCHAFT – SOCIÉTÉ IMMOBILIÈRE ■ 9 Client: SUNDANCE MESA Design Firm: A-HILL DESIGN Art Director/Designer: TOM ANTREASIAN Country: USA Business: REAL ESTATE DEVELOPER – IMMOBILIENGESELLSCHAFT – SOCIÉTÉ IMMOBILIÈRE ■ 10 Client: PATEFA GOLFING SOCIETY Design Firm: WATTS GRAPHIC DESIGN Art Directors/Designers: PETER WATTS, HELEN WATTS Photographer: PETER WATTS Country: AUSTRALIA Industry/Purpose: GOLF-CLUB (GOLF TRADE DAYS) – CLUB DE GOLF

1

2

3

4

5

6

7

8

9

1 Client: AMERICAN COUNCIL ON EXERCISE Design Firm: MIRES DESIGN, INC. Art Director/Designer: SCOTT MIRES Country: USA Description: EXERCISE CERTIFICATION MARK – ABZEICHEN FÜR AUSGEBILDETE SPORTTRAINER – INSIGNE POUR ENTRAINEURS DE SPORT PROFESSIONELS ■ 2 Client: UPPER DECK Design Firm: MIRES DESIGN, INC. Art Director/Designer: JOSE SERRANO Country: USA Description: BASKETBALL TRADING CARDS – POSTKARTEN MIT BASKETBALL-STARS – CARTES POSTALES AVEC LES STARS DU BASKET ■ 3 Client: SAN DIEGO HIKING CLUB Design Firm: MIRES DESIGN, INC. Art Director/Designer: JOSE SERRANO Country: USA Description: BACKPACKING AND HIKING CLUB – WANDERVEREIN – ASSOCIATION DES RANDONNEURS ■ 4 Client: LIMO VSETIN Design Firm: RM DESIGN Art Director/Designer: RADIM MOJZIS Country: CZECH REPUBLIC Description: SOFT DRINKS – ERFRISCHUNGSGETRÄNKE ■ 5 Client: BODE Design Firm: MIRES DESIGN, INC. Art Director/Designer: MIKE BROWER Country: USA Description:

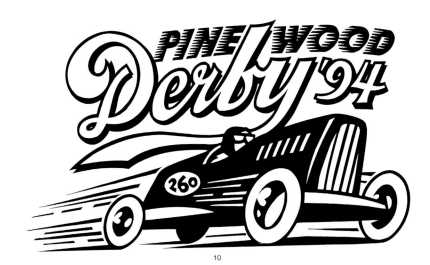

10

PERSONAL HEALTH AND FITNESS TRAINER – FITNESS-TRAINER – SANTÉ ET FITNESS ■ 6 Client: GOLFCLUB VELBERT GUT KUHLENDAHL E.V. Design Firm: DESIGN AHEAD Designer: RALF STUMPF Country: GERMANY Description: GOLF CLUB – CLUB DE GOLF ■ 7 Client: THE CROWN COMPANY Design Firm/Art Direction: FHA IMAGE DESIGN AUSTRALIA Design: FHA IMAGE DESIGN AUSTRALIA Country: AUSTRALIA, Description: ENTERTAINMENT COMPLEX WITH CASINO, HOTEL ETC., – GEBÄUDEKOMPLEX MIT KASINO, HOTEL ETC. ■ 8 Client: SUN INTERNATIONAL Design Firm: PENTAGRAPH DESIGN CONSULTANCY Art Director: MARK POSNETT Designer: ROBYN BAJKAI Country: SOUTH AFRICA Description: HOTEL GROUP – HOTELGRUPPE – GROUPE D'HÔTELS ■ 9 Client: UNIT-OFFICE Design Firm: *)MEDIAWERK Art Director: LUCAS BUCHHOLZ Designer: ZACHARIAS Country: GERMANY Description: DISCO – DISKOTHEK – DISCOTHÈQUE ■ 10 Client: PINEWOOD DERBY Design Firm: MIRES DESIGN, INC. Art Director/Designer: JOSE SERRANO Country: USA Description: ANNUAL BOY SCOUT DERBY – JÄHRLICHES PFADFINDER-DERBY – DERBY ANNUEL DES SCOUTS

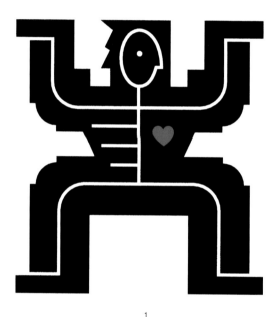

1

1 CLIENT: CHARLES JAMES DESIGN FIRM: SIBLEY/PETEET DESIGN ART DIRECTOR/DESIGNER/ILLUSTRATOR: DAVID BECK COUNTRY: USA DESCRIPTION: PERSONAL FITNESS TRAINER – FITNESS-TRAINER – FITNESS ∎ 2 CLIENT: TANZSCHULE HOCHSTÄTTER DESIGN FIRM: CHRISTINE PUCHNER - GRAPHIC-DESIGN ART DIRECTOR/DESIGNER: CHRISTINE PUCHNER COUNTRY: AUSTRIA DESCRIPTION: DANCE SCHOOL – TANZSCHULE – ÉCOLE DE DANSE

1

2

3

4

5

1 Client: PRIME RETAIL (INDIANA FACTORY SHOPS) Design Firm: JOSEPH RATTAN DESIGN Art Director: JOSEPH RATTAN Designer/Illustrator: DIANA MCKNIGHT Country: USA Description: WHOLESALE, RETAIL OUTLET – SHOPPING CENTER – GROSSHANDEL – COMMERCE DE GROS – CENTRE COMMERCIAL ■ **2** Client: HUTCHINSON PROPERTIES Design Firm: PPA DESIGN LIMITED Art Director/Designer: BYRON JACOBS Illustrators: BYRON JACOBS, PATRICK CHAN Country: HONG KONG Description: GRANDVIEW ENTERTAIN-MENT SHOPPING MALL – EINKAUFSZENTRUM – CENTRE COMMERCIAL ■ **3** Client: PRIME RETAIL (FLORIDA KEYS FACTORY SHOPS) Design Firm: JOSEPH RATTAN DESIGN Art Director: JOSEPH RATTAN Designer: GREG MORGAN Illustrator: GREG MORGAN Country: USA Description: WHOLESALE, RETAIL OUTLET

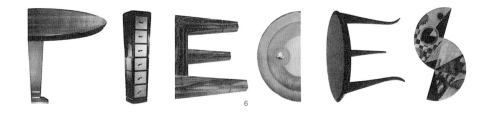

6

SHOPPING CENTER – GROSSHANDEL – COMMERCE DE GROS – CENTRE COMMERCIAL ■ **4** Client: MINIPREIS-MARKT LINZ Art Director/Designer: BORIS BERGHAMMER Country: AUSTRIA Description: SUPERMARKET – SUPERMARKT – SUPERMARCHÉ ■ **5** Client: PRIME RETAIL (GULFPORT FACTORY SHOPS) Design Firm: JOSEPH RATTAN DESIGN Art Director: JOSEPH RATTAN Designer/Illustrator: DIANA MCKNIGHT Country: USA Description: WHOLESALE, RETAIL OUTLET – SHOPPING CENTER – GROSSHANDEL – COMMERCE DE GROS – CENTRE COMMERCIAL ■ **6** Client: PIECES Design Firm: COY, LOS ANGELES Art Director: JOHN COY Designers: JOHN COY, MICHAEL DEAN HACKETT, ALBERT CHOI Country: USA Description: LIMITED EDITION FURNI-TURE MANUFACTURER – HERSTELLER VON MÖBEL-EDITIONEN – FABRICANT DE MEUBLES EN SÉRIE LIMITÉE

1 CLIENT: NINGBO THREE DESIGN FIRM: ART & DESIGN DEPT. SHANTOU UNIVERSITY ART DIRECTOR/DESIGNER: CHEN FANG ILLUSTRATOR: CHEN FANG COUNTRY: CHINA DESCRIPTION: PLAYING CARD COMPANY – SPIELKARTENHERSTELLER – FABRICANT DE JEUX DE CARTES ■ 2 CLIENT: GREEN ACRES DESIGN FIRM: GRETEMAN GROUP DESIGNER: SONIA GRETEMAN COUNTRY: USA DESCRIPTION: HEALTH FOOD STORE – REFORMHAUS – MAGASIN DE PRODUITS DIÉTIQUES ■ 3 CLIENT: HILL PARTNERS DESIGN FIRM: ANTISTA FAIRCLOUGH DESIGN ART DIRECTOR/ DESIGNER: THOMAS FAIRCLOUGH COUNTRY: USA DESCRIPTION:

1

CLIENT: MARINA CYCLERY ART DIRECTOR/DESIGNER: GRANT PETERSON COUNTRY: USA DESCRIPTION: BICYCLE STORE – FAHRRADLADEN – MAGASIN DE CYCLES ■ 5 CLIENT: PISTOL AND BURNES COFFEE COMPANY DESIGN FIRM: ANTISTA FAIRCLOUGH DESIGN ART DIRECTOR/DESIGNER: TOM ANTISTA COUNTRY: USA DESCRIPTION: COFFEE – KAFFEE – CAFÉ ■ 6 CLIENT: MONT SOURCE, INC. DESIGN FIRM: ANTISTA FAIRCLOUGH DESIGN ART DIRECTORS/ DESIGNERS: TOM ANTISTA, THOMAS FAIRCLOUGH ILLUSTRATOR: FLATLANDS COUNTRY: USA DESCRIPTION: MEN'S SKIN CARE PRODUCTS – KOSMETIKPRODUKTE FÜR MÄNNER – PRODUITS COSMÉTIQUES POUR HOMMES

2

3

4

5

6

1 CLIENT: WHIM WHAM PRODUCTIONS DESIGN FIRM: TANAGRAM ART DIRECTOR: ANTHONY MA DESIGNER/ILLUSTRATOR: GRANT DAVIS COUNTRY: USA DESCRIPTION: CHILDREN'S PRODUCTS — KINDERARTIKEL — ARTICLES POUR ENFANTS ■ 2 CLIENT: AQUAPENN SPRING WATER CO. DESIGN FIRM: SOMMESE DESIGN ART DIRECTORS: KRISTIN SOMMESE, LANNY SOMMESE DESIGNER: KRISTIN SOMMESE ILLUSTRATOR: LANNY SOMMESE COUNTRY: USA DESCRIPTION: SPRING WATER BRAND — MINERALWASSERMARKE — MARQUE DE FONTAINES ■ 3 CLIENT: DREAMMAKER CUSTOMS DESIGN FIRM: MIRES DESIGN, INC. ART DIRECTOR/DESIGNER: JOSÉ SERRANO ILLUSTRATOR: TRACY SABIN COUNTRY: USA DESCRIPTION: STREET WEAR CLOTHING — STRASSENBEKLEIDUNG — LIGNE DE STREET WEAR ■ 4 CLIENT: OBJEX DESIGN FIRM: JON FLAMING DESIGN ART DIRECTOR/DESIGNER: JON FLAMING COUNTRY: USA DESCRIPTION: ENVIRONMENTALLY CONSCIOUS HOME ACCESSORIES AND GIFT ITEMS — UMWELTVERTRÄGLICHE EINRICHTUNGSGEGENSTÄNDE UND GESCHENKE — ACCESSOIRES D'AMÉNAGEMENT ET ARTICLES CADEAU RESPECTUEUX DE L'ENVIRONNEMENT ■ 5 CLIENT: HEXAGRAPH FLY RODS COMPANY DESIGN FIRM: SWIETER DESIGN UNITED STATES ART DIRECTOR/DESIGNER: JOHN SWIETER COUNTRY: USA DESCRIPTION: FISHING RODS — ANGELN — CANNES À PÊCHE ■ 6 CLIENT: NIDECKER DESIGN FIRM: TINGUELY CONCEPT DESIGNER: JOHANN TERRETTAZ COUNTRY: SWITZERLAND DESCRIPTION: SNOWBOARDS ■ 7 CLIENT: CHUMS DESIGN FIRM: DUFFY DESIGN ART DIRECTOR: KOBE DESIGNERS/ILLUSTRATOR: KOBE, ALAN LEUSINK COUNTRY: USA DESCRIPTION: EYEGLASS RETENTION DEVICES AND CLOTHING LINE ■ 8 CLIENT: BEER BOY ENTERPRISES DESIGN FIRM: MACVICAR DESIGN AND COMMUNICATIONS ART DIRECTOR/DESIGNER/ILLUSTRATOR: JOHN VANCE COUNTRY: USA DESCRIPTION: RETAILER OF BEER BREWING KITS — VERKAUF VON GERÄTEN FÜR

1

DIE PRIVATE BIERBRAUEREI — VENTE EN DÉTAIL D'ARTICLES DU PARFAIT PETITS BRASSEUR. ■ 9 CLIENT: START TO FINISH BICYCLE SHOPS DESIGN FIRM: LANDKAMER HAMER DESIGN ART DIRECTOR/DESIGNER: MARK LANDKAMER COUNTRY: USA DESCRIPTION: BICYCLE SHOP — FAHRRADLADEN — MAGASIN DE CYCLES ■ 10 CLIENT: LOPEZ ELECTRIC DESIGN FIRM: BRIGHT & ASSOCIATES DESIGNER: KONRAD BRIGHT COUNTRY: USA DESCRIPTION: ELECTRIC — ELEKTRISCHE GERÄTE — APPAREILS ÉLECTRIQUES ■ 11 CLIENT: WAREHOUSE ROW FACTORY SHOPS DESIGN FIRM: JOSEPH RATTAN DESIGN ART DIRECTOR: JOSEPH RATTAN DESIGNER: DIANA MCKNIGHT COUNTRY: USA DESCRIPTION: WHOLESALE AND RETAIL OUTLET SHOPPING CENTER — GROSSHANDEL — COMMERCE EN GROS — CENTRE COMMERCIAL ■ 12 CLIENT: ARIZONA AUTO LEATHER DESIGN FIRM: C. KIM DESIGN & ADVERTISING ART DIRECTOR: CATHARINE M. KIM DESIGNERS/ILLUSTRATORS: CATHARINE M. KIM, KERRY MARTYR COUNTRY: USA DESCRIPTION: LEATHER AUTOMOTIVE ACCESSORIES — LEDERAUSSTATTUNGEN FÜR AUTOS — ACCESSOIRES ET ÉQUIPEMENT EN CUIR POUR VOITURES ■ 13 CLIENT: BÜRO-BEDARF THURNHER DESIGN FIRM: MOTTER-DESIGN DESIGNER: OTHMAR MOTTER COUNTRY: AUSTRIA DESCRIPTION: OFFICE SUPPLIES — BÜROBEDARF — ARTICLES DE BUREAUX ■ 14 CLIENT: VIAMED DESIGN FIRM/DESIGNER: RUNYAN HINSCHE ASSOCIATES ART DIRECTOR: JIM BERTE COUNTRY: USA DESCRIPTION: MEDICAL PRODUCTS — MEDIZINISCHE PRODUKTE — PRODUITS MÉDICAUX ■ 15 CLIENT: LASKA DESIGN FIRM: LTD "DESIGN-STUDIO 60 X 90" DESIGNER: SERGEI SARKISOV COUNTRY: RUSSIA DESCRIPTION: CONSUMER GOODS MANUFACTURING — HERSTELLUNG VON KONSUMGÜTERN — FABRICANT DE PRODUITS DE CONSOMMATION ■ 16 CLIENT: CHARLES BUTTON COMPANY DESIGN FIRM: SUPON DESIGN GROUP, INC. CREATIVE DIRECTOR: SUPON PHORNIRUNLIT COUNTRY: USA DESCRIPTION: BUTTON MANUFACTURER — HERSTELLER VON KNÖPFEN — FABRICANTS DE BOUTONS

2

3

4

5

6

7

8

9

10

11

12

13

14

15

16

1

2

PΣGΛSUS

3

4

5

1

2

3

4

5

1 Client: HABITAT FOR HUMANITY Design Firm: JOSEPH RATTAN DESIGN Art Director: JOSEPH RATTAN Designer: JOSEPH RATTAN, ALAN COLVIN Country: USA Description: VOLUNTEER ORGANIZATION BUILDING HOMES – FREIWILLIGEN-ORGANISATION, DIE HÄUSER BAUT – ENTREPRISE DE CONSTRUCTION BÉNÉVOLE. ■ 2 Client: DUBUQUE AREA CHAMBER OF COMMERCE Design Firm: MCCULLOUGH CREATIVE RESOURCES, INC. Art Director: JACK MCCULLOUGH Designer: MICHAEL SCHMALZ Country: USA Description: CHAMBER OF COMMERCE – HANDELSKAMMER – CHAMBRE DU COMMERCE ■ 3 Client: LAWRENCE CHAN WEDDING SERVICES CENTRE Design Firm: A. STUDIO & ASSOCIATES Art Director: SHU SUNG WAN Designer/Concept/Computer

6

Effect: JOSEPH YIM CHI HANG Country: HONG KONG Description: WEDDING SERVICE – HOCHZEITS-SERVICE – SERVICE MATRIMONIAL ■ 4 Client: FIRST CONGREGATIONAL CHURCH Design Firm: JOSEPH RATTAN DESIGN Art Director/Designer: JOSEPH RATTAN Country: USA Description: CHURCH – KIRCHE – ÉGLISE ■ 5 Client: AKI Design Firm: MUI + GRAY Art Director/Designer: KAI MUI Country: ITALY Description: SPORTWEAR COMPANY'S SOCIAL AWARENESS CAMPAIGN – SOZIALES ANLIEGEN EINES SPORTARTIKELHERSTELLERS – CAMPAGNE À CARACTÈRE SOCIAL D'UN FABRICANT D'ARTICLES DE SPORT ■ 6 Client: UNITED TECHNOLOGIES CORPORATION Design Firm: POLLARD DESIGN Art Director/Designer: JEFF POLLARD Country: USA Description: ANNUAL REPORT ON CORPORATE GIVING – JAHRESBERICHT ÜBER FIRMENSPENDEN – RAPPORT ANNUEL DE DONS D'ENTREPRISE

Boulder Ridge

1

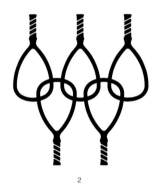

2

3

1 Client: BOULDER RIDGE Design Firm: COAKLEY HEAGERTY Art Director: J.D. KESER Designer/Illustrator: MICHAEL SCHWAB Country: USA Description: GOLF COURSE – GOLFPLATZ – TERRAIN DE GOLF ■ **2** Client: EKTELON Design Firm: MIRES DESIGN Art Director/Designer: JOSE SERRANO Country: USA Description: OLYMPIC TEAM IDENTITY – IDENTITÄT FÜR DIE OLYMPIA-MANNSCHAFT – LOGO POUR L'ÉQUIPE OLYMPIQUE ■ **3** Client:

4

YMCA Design Firm: MIRES DESIGN Art Director/Designer: JOSE SERRANO Country: USA Description: INTER-NATIONAL ROWING AND PADDLING REGATTA – INTERNATIONALE RUDER- UND PADDEL-REGATTA – RÉGALE INTER-NATIONALE À L'AVIRON ■ **4** Client: HAPPY SAILING Design Firm: ARNO SCHMID DESIGN Art Director/Designer/Illustrator: ARNO SCHMID Country: SWITZERLAND Description: SAILING CLUB – SEGELVEREIN – CLUB DE VOILE

1 CLIENT: NIKE, INC. DESIGN FIRM: MIRES DESIGN, INC. ART DIRECTOR/DESIGNER: SCOTT MIRES COUNTRY: USA DESCRIPTION: FITNESS SHOE, APPAREL – FITNESS SCHUHE UND BEKLEIDUNG – CHAUSSURE ET SURVÊTEMENTS DE FITNESS ■ 2 CLIENT: TRI-BAN E.V. DESIGN FIRM: GIRAFFE WERBEAGENTUR DESIGNER: SAMI HOKKANEN COUNTRY: GERMANY DESCRIPTION: TRIATHLON ASSOCIATION – TRIATHLON-VEREIN – CLUB DE TRIATHLON ■ 3 CLIENT: SMTI, INC. DESIGN FIRM: GERARD HUERTA DESIGN, INC. ART DIRECTORS: BARBARA ROSENWACH, MIKE LETIS, BOB O'CONNOR DESIGNER/ILLUSTRATOR: GERARD HUERTA COUNTRY: USA DESCRIPTION: "BREEDERS' CUP '95" – ZÜCHTER-CUP '95 – COUPE DES ÉLEVEURS '95 ■ 4 CLIENT: TURKISH ARCHERY FEDERATION ART DIRECTOR/DESIGNER: BÜLENT ERKMEN COUNTRY: TURKEY DESCRIPTION: ARCHERY CHAMPIONSHIP – MEISTERSCHAFT IM BOGENSCHIESSEN ■ 5 CLIENT: FUSSBALLCLUB HARD DESIGN FIRM: MOTTER-DESIGN DESIGNER: OTHMAR MOTTER COUNTRY: AUSTRIA DESCRIPTION: SOCCER TEAM – FUSSBALLCLUB – CLUB DE FOOTBALL ■ 6 CLIENT: THE LIPTON CHAMPIONSHIPS DESIGN FIRM: PINKHAUS DESIGN ART DIRECTORS: JOHN NORMAN, SUSIE LAWSON, JOEL FULLER DESIGNER – ILLUSTRATOR: JOHN NORMAN COUNTRY: USA DESCRIPTION: TENNIS TOURNAMENT – TENNISTURNIER – TOURNOI DE TENNIS ■ 7 CLIENT: P.M.S. LIMITED DESIGN FIRM: CARTER WONG + PARTNERS ART DIRECTOR: NICK DOWNES DESIGNER: TOBY GLOVER ILLUSTRATOR: ROBIN CARTER COUNTRY: GREAT BRITAIN DESCRIPTION: POLO TEAM – POLO-MANNSCHAFT – EQUIPE DE POLO ■ 8 CLIENT: SOCCER UNITED DESIGN FIRM: RBMM/THE RICHARDS GROUP ART DIRECTOR/DESIGNER: HORACIO COBOS ILLUSTRATORS: HORACIO COBOS, WAYNE JOHNSON COUNTRY: USA DESCRIPTION: SOCCER INSTRUCTIONAL METHOD – FUSSBALL-TRAININGSMETHODE – MÉTHODE D'ENTRAÎNEMENT AU FOOTBALL ■ 9 CLIENT: NIKE, INC.

1

DESIGN FIRM: NIKE DESIGN DESIGNER: ALAN COLVIN COUNTRY: USA DESCRIPTION: ATHLETIC FOOTWEAR, SPORTS COMPETITION – SCHUHE FÜR LEICHTATHLETIK, SPORTVERANSTALTUNG – CHAUSSURES D'ATHLÉTISME, MANIFESTATION SPORTIVE ■ 10 CLIENT: CLEATS & CLEAVAGE DESIGN FIRM: SIBLEY/PETEET DESIGN ART DIRECTOR/DESIGNER/ILLUSTRATOR: DONNA ALDRIDGE COUNTRY: USA DESCRIPTION: WOMEN'S SOCCER TEAM – FRAUEN-FUSSBALLTEAM – EQUIPE DE FOOTBALLEUSES ■ 11 CLIENT: BOKSACKI KLUB "LEONARDO" ART DIRECTOR/DESIGNER/ILLUSTRATOR: IVICA BELINIC COUNTRY: CROATIA DESCRIPTION: BOXING CLUB – BOX-CLUB – CLUB DE BOXE ■ 12 CLIENT: TOM LANDRY SPORTS TEAM DESIGN FIRM: SWIETER DESIGN UNITED STATES ART DIRECTOR: JOHN SWIETER DESIGNER: PAUL MUNSTERMAN COUNTRY: USA DESCRIPTION: SPORTS TEAM – SPORTCLUB – CLUB DE SPORT ■ 13 CLIENT: RIOT V DESIGN FIRM: FACTOR DESIGN ART DIRECTOR: RÜDIGER GÖTZ DESIGNER/ILLUSTRATOR: RÜDIGER GÖTZ COUNTRY: GERMANY DESCRIPTION: BASEBALL CAP – BASEBALLMÜTZE – CASQUETTE DE BASEBALL ■ 14 CLIENT: BALTIC KÖLLN DESIGN FIRM: FACTOR DESIGN ART DIRECTOR/DESIGNER/ILLUSTRATOR: RÜDIGER GÖTZ COUNTRY: GERMANY DESCRIPTION: RETAIL CHAIN FOR WATER SPORTS EQUIPMENT – WASSERSPORT-FACHGESCHÄFTSKETTE – CHAÎNE DE MAGASINS D'ÉQUIPEMENTS POUR SPORTS AQUATIQUES ■ 15 CLIENT: CAPITAL BASKETBALL LTD. DESIGN FIRM: BNA DESIGN ART DIRECTOR: GRENVILLE MAIN DESIGNER/ILLUSTRATOR: DIANA BIDWELL COUNTRY: NEW ZEALAND DESCRIPTION: BASKETBALL TEAM – EQUIPE DE BASKET ■ 16 CLIENT: NIKE, INC. DESIGN FIRM: NIKE DESIGN ART DIRECTOR/DESIGNER: DAN RICHARDS COUNTRY: USA DESCRIPTION: OREGON STATE TENNIS CHAMPIONSHIP – TENNISTURNIER VON OREGON – TOURNOI DE TENNIS

2

3

4

5

6

7

8

9

10

11

12

13

14

15

16

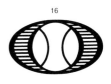

1

2

1 CLIENT: CHAMPION LEAGUE SPORTS DESIGN FIRM: LATITUDE/THE RICHARDS GROUP ART DIRECTOR: FELIX P. STOCKWELL COUNTRY: USA DESCRIPTION: SPORTS LEAGUE – SPORTLIGA – DIVISION DE SPORT ■ 2 CLIENT: COCHISE COUNTY CYCLING CLASSIC DESIGN FIRM: PORTFOLIO CENTER DESIGNER: JAY SHOEMAKE COUNTRY: USA DESCRIPTION: BIKE RACE – FAHRRADRENNEN – VÉLOS DE COURSE ■ 3 CLIENT: ROYAL HONG KONG YACHT CLUB DESIGN FIRM: PPA DESIGN LIMITED ART DIRECTOR: BYRON JACOBS DESIGNER: BYRON JACOBS COUNTRY: HONG KONG DESCRIPTION: ROYAL HONG KONG YACHT CLUB 100 YEARS COMMEMORATIVE – 100 JAHRE JACHTKLUB VON HONGKONG – CENTENAIRE DU YACHT-CLUB DE HONG KONG

TM

EXTREME
technologies

2

3

4

5

6

1 Client: LTV & COMPANY Design Firm: TOLLESON DESIGN Art Director: STEVE TOLLESON Designers: STEVE TOLLESON, CHASE WATTS Country: USA Description: COMMUNICATIONS CORPORATION — KOMMUNIKATIONS-FIRMA — ENTREPRISE DE COMMUNICATION ■ **2** Client: SEGA CHANNEL Design Firm: BLACKDOG Art Director: MARK FOX Designer: MARK FOX Country: USA Description: CABLE CHANNEL — KABELKANAL — CHAÎNE CÂBLÉE ■ **3** Client: RIOT V Design Firm: FACTOR DESIGN Art Director/Designer/Illustrator: RÜDIGER GÖTZ Country: GERMANY Description: MOVIE PRODUCTION — FILMPRODUKTION — PRODUCTION DE FILMS ■ **4** Client: DOUGLAS PRODUCTIONS Design Firm: DOTZLER DESIGN Art Director: RAY DOTZLER Designer: TIM GRUTSCH Country: USA Description: VIDEO PRODUCTION COMPANY — VIDEO-PRODUKTIONEN — PRODUCTION DE VIDÉOS ■ **5** Client: PERFECTLY ROUND PRODUCTIONS Design Firm: GRETEMAN GROUP Art Director: SONIA GRETEMAN Designer: JAMES STRANGE Country: USA Description: FILM, VIDEO PRODUCTION COMPANY — FILM UND VIDEO-PRODUKTIONEN — PRODUCTION DE FILMS ET VIDÉOS ■ **6** Client/Design Firm: TRIAD, INC. Art Director: MICHAEL HINSHAW Country: USA Description: VIDEO FIELD TRIPS FOR CHILDREN — VIDEOSPIELE FÜR KINDER — JEUX VIDÉO POUR ENFANTS ■ **7** Client: SUNDOG PRODUCTIONS Design Firm: POLLARD DESIGN Art Director/Designer: JEFF POLLARD Country: USA Description: FILM AND VIDEO PRODUCTION COMPANY —

1

FILM UND VIDEO-PRODUKTIONEN — PRODUCTION DE FILMS ET VIDÉOS ■ **8** Client: SAN FRANCISCO PRODUCTION GROUP Design Firm: MORLA DESIGN Art Director: JENNIFER MORLA Designers: JENNIFER MORLA, CRAIG BAILEY Country: USA Description: VIDEO PRODUCTION FACILITY — STUDIO FÜR VIDEO-PRODUKTIONEN — STUDIO DE PRODUCTIONS VIDÉO ■ **9** Client: RADIOLAND Design Firm: SANDSTROM DESIGN Art Director/Designer: STEVEN SANDSTROM Illustrator: DONJIRO BAN Country: USA Description: RADIO ADVERTISING CREATIVE AND PRODUCTION — RADIOWERBUNG, KONZEPTION UND PRODUKTION — PUBLICITÉ RADIOPHONIQUE, CONCEPTION ET PRODUCTION ■ **10** Client: RPM VIDEO PRODUCTIONS Design Firm: ZAUHAR DESIGN Art Director/Designer/Illustrator: DAVID ZAUHAR Country: USA Description: VIDEO PRODUCTIONS — VIDEO-PRODUKTIONEN — PRODUCTIONS VIDÉO ■ **11** Client: GOLDMAN VIDEO Design Firm: FIREHOUSE 101 ART & DESIGN Art Director: LORI SIEBERT Designer/Illustrator: KIRK RICHARD SMITH Country: USA Description: VIDEO PRODUCTIONS — VIDEO-PRODUKTIONEN — PRODUCTIONS VIDÉO ■ **12** Client: PACIFICOM INTERNATIONAL Design Firm: FISHTALK DESIGN Art Director/Designer: EUGENE BUSTILLOS Country: USA Description: PRODUCTION COMPANY — PRODUKTIONSFIRMA — SOCIÉTÉ DE PRODUCTIONS ■ **13** Client: AVISTAR Design Firm: MARK ANDERSON DESIGN Art Director: MARK ANDERSON Designer: MARK SELFE Country: USA Description: VIDEO CONFERENCING COMPANY — VIDEO-KONFERENZEN — CONFÉRENCES VIDÉO

2

3

4

5

6

7

8

9

10

11

12

13

1

2

3

4

5

1 Client: BACKBONE Design Firm: BLACKDOG Designer/Illustrator: MARK FOX Country: USA Description: BLUES BAND ■ **2** Client: WATER PLANET/GOLD PHOTO LTD. Design Firm: PPA DESIGN LIMITED Art Director: BYRON JACOBS Designer/Illustrator: BYRON JACOBS Country: HONG KONG Description: FINE ART POSTERS AND BOOKS ON WATER-RELATED THEMES – KUNSTPLAKATE UND BÜCHER ZUM THEMA WASSER ■ **3** Client: CIRCA THEATRE Design Firm: BNA DESIGN Art Director: IAN NEWLANDS Designers: IAN NEWLANDS, SARAH WILLIAMS Illustrator: SIMON SHAW Country: NEW ZEALAND Description: DRAMA COMPANY PRODUCTION OF "ANGELS IN AMERICA" – THEATERPRODUKTION VON «ANGELS IN AMERICA» – PRODUCTION THÉÂTRALE DE «ANGELS OF AMERICA» ■ **4** Client: KAWAGUCHIKO STELLAR THEATER Design Firm: SHIN

6

MATSUNAGA DESIGN INC. Art Director/Designer: SHIN MATSUNAGA Country: JAPAN Description: OPEN-AIR THEATER – FREILICHTTHEATER – THÉÂTRE EN PLEIN AIR ■ **5** Client: SEATTLE REPERTORY THEATRE Design Firm: MODERN DOG Art Director: MICHAEL STRASSBURGER Designer: MICHAEL STRASSBURGER Country: USA Description: REPERTORY THEATRE – REPERTOIRE-THEATER – THÉÂTRE DE RÉPERTOIRE ■ **6** Client: PLAYHOUSE INTERNATIONAL PICTURES Design Firm: R/GREENBERG ASSOCIATES, INC. Art Director: MICHAEL RILEY Designers: GARSON YU, MICHAEL RILEY Illustrators: GARSON YU, MICHAEL RILEY Country: USA Description: DEVELOPMENT, PRODUCTION CO. – THEATERPRODUKTIONEN – PRODUCTIONS THÉÂTRALES

1

(THIS SPREAD) 1–6 Client: POST BANK, EXPRESS POST MAIL Design Firm: JELENA KITAJEVA ART DESIGN
STUDIO Art Director: JELENA KITAJEVA Designer: JELENA KITAJEVA Illustrator: JELENA KITAJEVA
Country: RUSSIA Description: EXPRESS MAIL SERVICE – EXPRESS-POSTDIENST – COURRIER EXPRÈS

2

3

4

5

6

1

2

3

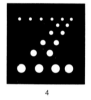

4

5

6

7

8

9

1 Client: GREAT WESTERN RAILWAYS COMPANY Design Firm: ROUNDEL DESIGN GROUP Art Director: MICHAEL DENNY Designers: DEBORAH OSBORNE, JOHN BATESON, HAROLD BATTEN Country: GREAT BRITAIN Description: RAILROAD COMPANY – EISENBAHNGESELLSCHAFT – COMPAGNIE DE CHEMINS DE FER ■ 2 Client: FEDERAL EXPRESS CORPORATION Design Firm: LANDOR ASSOCIATES Creative Director: COURTNEY REESER Art Director: LINDON GRAY LEADER Designers: WALLACE KRANTZ, BRUCE MCGOVERT, LINDON LEADER Country: USA Description: OVERNIGHT PACKAGE DELIVERY – KURIERDIENST – COURRIERS EXPRÉS ■ 3 Client: CITY OF TEMPE Design Firm: THINKING CAPS Art Director/Designer/Illustrator: ANN MORTON Country: USA Description: PUBLIC TRANSPORTATION SYSTEM – ÖFFENTLICHE VERKEHRSMITTEL – TRANS-PORTS PUBLICS ■ 4 Client: ZHUHAI AIRPORT Design Firm: YE DESIGN Art Director/Designer: XIAO YONG Country: CHINA Description: AIRPORT – FLUGHAFEN – AÉROPORT ■ 5 Client: GAVIN AIR Design Firm: KRAUS LEFEVRE STUDIOS Art Director: ROMAN KRAUS Designer: TIM DOYLE Country: USA Description: CUSTOM AIR SERVICE – PRIVATE FLUGLINIE – COMPAGNIE AÉRIENNE PRIVÉE ■ 6 Client: ZYNYX Design Firm:

10

BREMMER & GORIS COMMUNICATIONS Art Director: DENNIS GORIS Designer/Illustrator: PETER BUTTECALI Country: USA Description: NE RAILROAD SERVICE – EISENBAHN-SERVICE – MESSAGERIE FERRONVIAIRE ■ 7 Client: CONSOLIDATED COURIERS Design Firm: SWIETER DESIGN UNITED STATES Art Director: JOHN SWIETER Designers/Illustrators: JOHN SWIETER, PAUL MUNSTERMAN Country: USA Description: COURIER COMPANY – KURIERFIRMA – COURRIERS ■ 8 Client: THE ICELANDIC POSTAL AND TELECOMMUNICATIONS SERVICE Design Firm: GOTT FOLK ADVERTISING AGENCY Art Director: HLYNUR OLAFSSON Designer: KRISTIN THORA GUDBJARTSDOTTIR Country: ICELAND Description: OVERNIGHT PARCEL DELIVERY SERVICE – KURIERDIENST – COURRIER EXPRÉS ■ 9 Client: AXIAL LIMITED Design Firm: ROUNDEL DESIGN GROUP Art Director: MICHAEL DENNY Designer: ANDREW ROSS, JEREMY ROOTS, MICHÈLE BURY, JOHN BATESON Country: GREAT BRITAIN Description: AUTOMOTIVE LOGISTICS – LOGISTIK FÜR AUTOTRANSPORTE ■ 10 Client: SPRINT & PRODUCTION Design Firm: ART FORCE STUDIO Art Director/Designer/Illustrator: ATTILA SIMON Country: HUNGARY Description: MESSENGER SERVICE – KURIERDIENST – SERVICE DE MESSAGERIE

1

2

3

4

5

1 Client: NORWEGIAN CRUISE LINE Design Firm: CKS PARTNERS Art Director: JILL SAVINI Designer: KAREN SMIDTH Illustrator: KAREN SMIDTH Country: USA Description: CRUISE LINE – KREUZFAHRTLINIE – CROISIÈRES ■ **2** Client: GOLDEN GATE NATIONAL PARKS ASSOCIATION Design Firm: GOODBY SILVERSTEIN + PARTNERS Art Director: RICH SILVERSTEIN Designer/Illustrator: MICHAEL SCHWAB DESIGN Country: USA Description: NATIONAL PARKS – NATIONALPARKS – PARCS NATIONAUX ■ **3** Client: TRAVELFEST Design Firm: HIXO, INC. Art Director: MIKE HICKS Designer: MATT HECK Country: USA Description: TRAVEL SUPER-STORE – GESCHÄFT FÜR REISEAUSSTATTUNGEN – MAGASIN D'ARTICLES DE VOYAGES ■ **4** Client: MEXICAN

6

MINISTRY OF TOURISM Design Firm: GARZA GROUP COMMUNICATIONS Art Director: AGUSTIN GARZA Designer: AGUSTIN GARZA Country: USA Description: TOURISM TRADE SHOW ON MEXICO'S TOURISM – FACHMESSE FÜR TOURISMUS IN MEXIKO – SALON DU TOURISME À MEXICO ■ **5** Client: ROYAL CARIBBEAN CRUISE LINE Design Firm: PINKHAUS DESIGN CORP. Art Director: JOEL FULLER Designer: TODD HOUSER, JOEL FULLER Illustrator: TODD HOUSER Country: USA Description: CRUISE LINE – KREUZFAHRTLINIE – CROISIÈRES ■ **6** Client: IVAC CORPORATION Design Firm: MIRES DESIGN, INC. Art Director: SCOTT MIRES Designer: SCOTT MIRES Country: USA Description: TRAVEL INCENTIVE – REISELEITUNG – AGENCE DE VOYAGES

SEJIN TOURS

1

2

THE TOURISM BUREAU
REPUBLIC OF CHINA

3

4

5

6

7

8

9

1 Client: SEJIN TOURS Design Firm: DOOKIM DESIGN Art Director: DOO H. KIM Designers: DONGIL LEE, SEUNGHEE LEE Country: KOREA Description: TOUR COMPANY – REISEGESELLSCHAFT – AGENCE DE VOYAGES ■ 2 Client: LORD HOWE ISLAND BOARD Design Firm: HARCUS DESIGN Art Director: ANNETTE HARCUS Illustrator: ANNETTE HARCUS Designers: ANNETTE HARCUS, LUCY WALKER Country: AUSTRALIA Description: PALMS FOR INTERNATIONAL EXPORT – PALMEN FÜR DEN EXPORT – PALMIERS POUR L'EXPORT ■ 3 Advisor: JILL SAVINI Designer: I-HUA CHEN Country: USA Description: TOURISM BUREAU – REISEBÜRO – AGENCE DE VOYAGES ■ 4 Client: SIGLO 21 Design Firm: RBMM/THE RICHARDS GROUP Art Director: HORACIO COBOS Designer: HORACIO COBOS Country: HONDURAS Description: TRAVEL AGENCY – REISEBÜRO – AGENCE DE VOYAGES ■ 5 Client: SAK-VOYAGE TRAVEL AGENCY Design Firm: KITAJEVA ART-DESIGN STUDIO Art Director: JELENA KITAJEVA Designer: JELENA KITAJEVA Illustrator: JELENA KITAJEVA Country: RUSSIA Description: TRAVEL AGENCY – REISEBÜRO – AGENCE DE VOYAGES ■ 6 Client:

10

11

12

13

14

15

16

17

18

AGB REISID Design Firm: VAAL DESIGN Art Director: IVAR SAKK Designer: IVAR SAKK Illustrator: IVAR SAKK Country: ESTONIA Description: TRAVEL AGENCY – REISEBÜRO – AGENCE DE VOYAGES ■ 7 Client: VIRTUAL ADVENTURES Design Firm: KEN SHAFER DESIGN Art Director: KEN SHAFER Designer: KEN SHAFER Illustrator: KEN SHAFER Country: USA Description: TRAVEL AND DOCUMENTARY MULTIMEDIA DEVELOPER – MULTIMEDIA-DOKUMENTATIONEN IM REISEBEREICH – DOCUMENTATION MULTIMÉDIA DANS LE SECTEUR DES VOYAGES ■ 8 Client: K CLUB Design Firm: LAMBDA, S.R.L. Art Director: ADELAIDE ACERBI Country: ANTIGUA Description: VACATION-CLUB-HOTEL – FERIEN-CLUB-HOTEL ■ 9 Client: CITY AND COUNT OF DENVER Design Firm: ROBERT W. TAYLOR DESIGN, INC. Art Director: ROBERT W. TAYLOR Designers: ROBERT W. TAYLOR, CLYDE P. MASON Country: USA Description: AIRPORT – FLUGHAFEN – AÉROPORT ■ 10-18 Client: STATE OF IOWA Design Firm: SAYLES GRAPHIC DESIGN Art Director: JOHN SAYLES Designer: JOHN SAYLES Country: USA Description: STATE OF IOWA TOURISM DEPARTMENT

CLIENT: PLANET CONNECTIONS DESIGN FIRM: ALEJANDRO LÓPEZ DESIGN ART DIRECTOR: ALEJANDRO LÓPEZ

DESIGNER: ALEJANDRO LÓPEZ COUNTRY: USA BUSINESS: TRAVEL AGENCY – REISEBÜRO – AGENCE DE VOYAGES

INDEX

VERZEICHNIS

INDEX

CLIENTS

Clients

CLIENTS

Clients

GRAPHIS POSTER
GRAPHIS POSTER
GRAPHIS POSTER
GRAPHIS POSTER
GRAPHIS POSTER

POSTER

92
93
94
95

The Human Condition

Photojournalism 1995

MUSIC CDS

GRAPHIS MUSIC CDS

GRAPHIS LETTERHEAD
GRAPHIS LETTERHEAD
GRAPHIS LETTERHEAD
GRAPHIS LETTERHEAD

LETTERHEAD

3

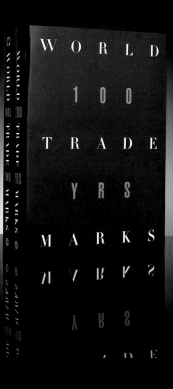

WORLD
100
TRADE
YRS
MARKS

GRAPHIS WORLD TRADE MARKS

DIGITAL FONTS

GRAPHIS DIGITAL FONTS

GRAPHIS STUDENT DESIGN

STUDENT DESIGN

GRAPHIS NEW MEDIA

NEW MEDIA

RICHARD SAUL WURMAN

INFORMATION ARCHITECTS

In·for·ma·tion Ar·chi·tect [L *info-tectus*] n. 1) the individual who organizes the patterns inherent in data, *making the complex clear.* 2) a person who creates the structure or map of information which allows others to find their personal path to knowledge. 3) the emerging 21st century professional occupation addressing the needs of the age focused upon clarity, human understanding and the science of the organization of information. -In·for·ma·tion Ar·chi·tec·ture

PETER BRADFORD *EDITOR*

G R A P H I S   B O O K S

BOOKS	USA/CANADA*	GERMANY	U.K.	ALL OTHER COUNTRIES
☐ GRAPHIS ADVERTISING 96	US$ 69.95	DM 149,–	£ 52.00	SFR. 123.–
☐ GRAPHIS ALTERNATIVE PHOTOGRAPHY 95	US$ 69.95	DM 149,–	£ 52.00	SFR. 123.–
☐ GRAPHIS ANNUAL REPORTS 4	US$ 69.95	DM 162,–	£ 55.00	SFR. 137.–
☐ GRAPHIS BOOK DESIGN	US$ 75.95	DM 162,–	£ 55.00	SFR. 137.–
☐ GRAPHIS CORPORATE IDENTITY 2	US$ 75.95	DM 162,–	£ 55.00	SFR. 137.–
☐ GRAPHIS DESIGN 96	US$ 69.95	DM 149,–	£ 52.00	SFR. 123.–
☐ GRAPHIS DIGITAL FONTS	US$ 69.95	DM 149,–	£ 52.00	SFR. 123.–
☐ GRAPHIS EPHEMERA	US$ 75.95	DM 162,–	£ 55.00	SFR. 137.–
☐ GRAPHIS FINE ART PHOTOGRAPHY	US$ 85.95	DM 155,–	£ 69.00	SFR. 128.–
☐ GRAPHIS INFORMATION ARCHITECTS	US$ 49.95	DM 149,–	£ 52.00	SFR. 123.–
☐ GRAPHIS LETTERHEAD 3	US$ 75.00	DM 162,–	£ 55.00	SFR. 137.–
☐ GRAPHIS LOGO 3	US$ 49.95	DM 149,–	£ 52.00	SFR. 123.–
☐ GRAPHIS MUSIC CDS	US$ 75.95	DM 162,–	£ 55.00	SFR. 137.–
☐ GRAPHIS NEW MEDIA	US$ 75.00	DM 162,–	£ 55.00	SFR. 137.–
☐ GRAPHIS NUDES (PAPERBACK)	US$ 39.95	DM 71,–	£ 32.00	SFR. 59.–
☐ GRAPHIS PHOTO 95	US$ 69.95	DM 149,–	£ 52.00	SFR. 123.–
☐ GRAPHIS POSTER 96	US$ 69.95	DM 149,–	£ 52.00	SFR. 123.–
☐ GRAPHIS PRODUCTS BY DESIGN	US$ 75.95	DM 149,–	£ 52.00	SFR. 123.–
☐ GRAPHIS SHOPPING BAGS	US$ 69.95	DM 149,–	£ 52.00	SFR. 123.–
☐ GRAPHIS STUDENT DESIGN 96	US$ 49.95	DM 71,–	£ 32.00	SFR. 59.–
☐ GRAPHIS TYPOGRAPHY 1	US$ 69.95	DM 162,–	£ 55.00	SFR. 137.–
☐ GRAPHIS TYPE SPECIMENS	US$ 49.95	DM 89,–	£ 37.00	SFR. 75.–
☐ **GRAPHIS PAPER SPECIFIER SYSTEM (GPS)**	US$495.00			

** ADD $30 SHIPPING/HANDLING FOR GPS

NOTE! NY RESIDENTS ADD 8.25% SALES TAX

☐   CHECK ENCLOSED (PAYABLE TO GRAPHIS)

☐   CHARGE MY CREDIT CARD:

☐ AMERICAN EXPRESS

☐ MASTERCARD/EUROCARD/ACCESS

☐ VISA/BARCLAYCARD/CARTE BLEUE

(FOR ORDERS FROM EC COUNTRIES V.A.T. WILL BE CHARGED

CARD NO.   EXP. DATE

CARDHOLDER NAME

SIGNATURE

(PLEASE PRINT)

NAME

COMPANY

ADDRESS

CITY

STATE/PROVINCE   ZIP CODE

COUNTRY

SEND ORDER FORM AND MAKE CHECK PAYABLE TO:
GRAPHIS US, INC.,
141 LEXINGTON AVENUE, NEW YORK, NY 10016-8193, USA

PLEASE SEND ORDER FORM TO:
GRAPHIS PRESS CORP.
DUFOURSTRASSE 107, CH–8008 ZÜRICH, SWITZERLAND

Graphis 296

The Digital Revolution: R/GA Softimage Silicon Graphics European Mindscapes Multimedia

Graphis 295

Carson Chiat/Day Apeloig Leith Agency Legorreta Gorham

Ishioka Fletcher Arnett ABV Achilli & Piazza CD Boxed Sets

G R A P H I S   M A G A Z I N E

MAGAZINE	USA	CANADA	SOUTHAMERICA/ ASIA/PACIFIC	GERMANY	U.K.	ALL OTHER COUNTRIES
☐ ONE YEAR (6 ISSUES)	US$ 89.00	US$ 99.00	US$ 125.00	DM 190,–	£ 68.00	SFR. 164.–
☐ TWO YEARS (12 ISSUES)	US$ 159.00	US$ 179.00	US$ 235.00	DM 342,–	£ 122.00	SFR. 295.–
☐ AIRMAIL SURCHARGE (6 ISSUES)	US$ 59.00	US$ 59.00	US$ 59.00	DM 75,–	£ 30.00	SFR 65.–
☐ REGISTERED MAIL				DM 24,–	£ 9.00	SFR 20.–

☐ 25% DISCOUNT FOR STUDENTS WITH COPY OF VALID,
   DATED STUDENT ID AND PAYMENT WITH ORDER

☐ CHECK ENCLOSED   (PAYABLE TO GRAPHIS)

☐ CHARGE MY CREDIT CARD:

☐ AMERICAN EXPRESS

☐ MASTERCARD/EUROCARD/ACCESS

☐ VISA/BARCLAYCARD/CARTE BLEUE

CARD NO.   EXP. DATE

CARDHOLDER NAME

SIGNATURE

☐ PLEASE BILL ME

(PLEASE PRINT)

NAME

TITLE

COMPANY

ADDRESS

CITY

STATE/PROVINCE   ZIP CODE

COUNTRY

SEND ORDER FORM AND MAKE CHECK PAYABLE TO:
GRAPHIS US, INC.,
141 LEXINGTON AVENUE, NEW YORK, NY 10016-8193, USA

PLEASE SEND ORDER FORM TO:
GRAPHIS PRESS CORP.
DUFOURSTRASSE 107, CH–8008 ZÜRICH, SWITZERLAND

SERVICE BEGINS WITH ISSUE THAT IS CURRENT WHEN ORDER IS PROCESSED.